FINDING GOD IN HOLLYWOOD

Discovering the Divine in Films, Movie Stars, & Stories

By Nathan Clarkson

Originate Press

Finding God in Hollywood: Discovering the Divine in
Films, Movie Stars, & Stories
By Originate Press
Copyright 2023 Nathan Clarkson

ISBN 979-8-9872819-1-8

"Nathan Clarkson captures the desperate disappointment so many have in Hollywood and Christianity, which both promise us everything, yet so often seemingly don't deliver, and gives a moving plea on how both can do better. This is required reading for anyone who's had their heart captured by either God or Hollywood."

- **Joseph Holmes** *Film critic for Religion Unplugged, filmmaker, co-host of The Overthinkers podcast*

"Like all good storytellers, Nathan ushers you into a world you haven't experienced. Like all faithful believers, he points out God along the way. Whether you faithfully follow Jesus, are daring to hope God is real, or are just curious about an actor's journey, *Finding God in Hollywood* will give you a glimpse inside the soul of an artist and the heart of God."

- **Chris Greer** *Former actor and pastor in Los Angeles, retreat leader, and author of 12 Rules for a Christian Life*

"Finding God in Hollywood is a must read for anyone trying to find truth and greater meaning in the arts — especially the film industry. Nathan is wise beyond his years and I admire his ability to be honest, encouraging, and inspiring in his books. This is my favorite book from Nathan yet and I think it will have a huge and lasting impact."

- **Spencer Folmar** *Award winning filmmaker of Generational Sins, Shooting Heroin. CEO of Hard Faith Films*

"Hollywood is simultaneously messy and beautiful. And so are we. What Nathan has done here is tie the two together with refreshing transparency. On top of it, he brings a bigger, better story -- God's story -- into the picture. The result, *Finding God in Hollywood*, is an easy but meaningful read -- one that takes us inside one man's dreams, desires and divine inspiration within an industry of mythmaking."

- **Cody Benjamin** *Author of Movies from the Mountaintop, staff writer at Paramount/CBS Sports*

"*Finding God in Hollywood* is a must-read for any believer who wants to or already works in film and television, whether in front of or behind the camera. It's a celebration of cinematic storytelling juxtaposed with biblical truths. Nathan's collection of candid anecdotes are fascinating and heartbreaking, providing both profound and necessary lessons for the Christian who creates."

-   **Chris Pierdomenico** *Filmmaker, podcaster, teacher, and Dork-in-Chief at DorkDaily.com*

"This book is a stellar read altogether. It helped me to understand that the beauty of God is inescapable. If you are a Chrisitian that loves movies and the art of filmmaking, this is the perfect book for you!"

-   **Craig Brown** *Director, producer, writer of film Shooting Doves*

"An engrossing read for any who love both their faith and their films."

-   **Louis Giovino** *Film producer, talent manager*

Nathan Clarkson is unwavering, sharing his warts and all experience as both a Christian and an artist pursuing a calling in the Hollywood system. How do we navigate one of the toughest industries in the world while staying grounded in our faith? How do we represent Christ well when struggling to pursue our dreams? Not only is this a must read for any Christian looking to work in the entertainment industry but the questions and lessons are universal to any person of faith pursuing a calling set on their hearts.

- **Benjamin Ironside Koppin** *Writer, director of Pastor's Kid, Kill A Prophet, Return to Me*

"Nathan delves into the Hollywood mystique and shows you can still find beauty, hope, goodness, and triumph through God's presence."

- **Jonathan Graham** *Former news producer, church pastor, and MLB chaplain. Vice President of Master Media International*

To all the storytellers

Before there were city lights spotlighting fancy soft drink ads and billboards for the upcoming superhero flick, before there were film lights on movie sets inside large studios shining on the faces of young starlets and hopeful actors telling the stories of our time, before there were fluorescent lights in my studio apartment illuminating my dark nights of the soul longing for purpose, there were lights in the sky.

There were lights cast across the vast cosmos, revealing the heavens, setting the stage for the story of all of history to begin its scene; stars showing the props in the form of planets, each reflecting back to the grandeur and brilliance of their creator.

The stars in heaven and the stars in Hollywood both shine boldly as evidence of the importance of story, and more importantly, the story that each of us have a part in.

Introduction

The Hollywood Story

"If God doesn't destroy Hollywood Boulevard, he owes Sodom and Gomorah an apology."

- Jay Leno

Movies like *Once Upon a Time in Hollywood*, *La La Land*, and *Singin' in the Rain* are all fantasies, each filled with colorful characters, hypnotic settings, and soundtracks that make us feel as if anything we did beneath them would be meaningful. But before I ever stepped foot in the City of Angels, I believed movies like this to be not fiction, but documentary – one I wanted so badly to be a part of. I wanted the swirling magic of the entertainment industry to make me one of its players, I wanted to feel the jealousy of the people who were not invited into its city limits, and I wanted ultimately to make myself immortal, so I

1

would have no need for God. So I believed this fantasy I had seen on screens and postcards, I believed the poetic words I read about this place and listened to in songs. But what I found was a world much different than I had hoped – one filled with desperation, despair, shame, strip malls, and littered streets. A far cry from the vision that had been cast for me inside my head.

Freshly out of my teens, having finished acting school in New York City, I decided it was time to make my move to Los Angeles. After a cross-country trip with a girl I liked (who I haven't spoken to in years), I found myself living in the Hollywood Hills, in a very rich friend's house. The landlord told us rumors about it having been Steve McQueen's old home, showing us all the hiding places around the home where classic movie stars would hide their drugs.

At night, through the thin doors, I would hear all sorts of noises from the parade of people my friend's money would attract – men doing drugs and vulnerable women making mistakes with said men. One morning he asked me to drive one of the women home, as he hadn't yet sobered up. On the drive she seemed sad and ashamed. I tried to say things to make her laugh.

After a month, I decided to find a new place. The morning I left, I found my friend downstairs, sitting at the dining room table, looking intently at a line of white powder.

"I need to stop," he said, looking up at me with a defeated and tired smile.

"You can, right now. Just make the choice," I told him. He laughed, bowed his head down, and snorted his self-medication.

I got in my car and left with both the sudden and month-long realization that the movies had told me a lie.

After moving into an apartment with four other poor actors like me, I found myself working as an extra or "background artist," making sixty-four dollars a day to be a blur in the background of movies and TV Shows. At least there I'd be a part, albeit a blurry one, of this industry of dreams I was chasing. It paid the rent.

It was there, as an extra on set for sometimes fifteen hours a day, that I found out all of the magic that lives on theater screens and in the pages of magazines is just a trick that hides the hectic, anxious, and tired life of a set, behind its edited and colored scenes. I found out my favorite actors were sad, my favorite scenes were special effects, and the sparkly world of entertainment was almost entirely made up.

In the coming years, I felt, over and over, both the desperation to see if this town would make good on its promises and the continual realization that it never intended to. It had lied to me and the millions of other souls who came searching for its rewards. Like an evil and beautiful succubus straight out of ancient myths, it lures young souls in with promises of pleasure and fulfillment, right into their ultimate demise, devouring them so she can keep her power while taking their lives.

More than a decade later, I still find myself wishing the town I see on the screen in movies like *La La Land* was real, a land filled with rich colors, choreographed dance numbers, and happy endings. But the lines on my forehead hold the hard-earned sense to know it's simply not true. Ironically enough, the most accurate on-screen depiction of Hollywood I've ever seen is a cartoon where the characters are all dysfunctional animals.

The world we live in is filled with things that *look* enchanting, like inhumanly smooth swimsuit models on social media, miracle pills on late-night TV, and instant gratification to our every whim with only the swipe of an app. Each of these things tells us a story – a story about reality, a story about ourselves, a story we so desire to be true. But behind each of these seemingly perfect things lies a dark, disappointing reality, filled with blemishes, side effects, and slow deaths that we ignore for the more beautiful lie.

But why do we believe them? Why do we buy into these tales that, deep down, we know are too good to be true? Could it be that we were made to long for a better story than the one we're telling now? And could it be that Hollywood has capitalized on that intrinsic human proclivity for gain?

Maybe it's God's fault. He made us like this. He made us to want the world to be better than it is. He made us to want *ourselves* to be better than we are. He made us to desire good stories. He designed us with hearts that tell us, even in the midst of a world that is falling apart, there is good to be found. The yearning to be a part of and believe in good stories is one that is embedded in our hearts, minds, and souls. God has placed a longing to not only love and connect to a good story, but to be a part of one, like actors in a movie. And like any good story, Hollywood shows us what we wish the world could be and who we wish we were.

God isn't mentioned often in Hollywood, and when He is, it's usually as a joke or a way to sell something. A talent manager once asked me if I believed in God. I told him I did, and he replied, "I'm your God now." But I knew he wasn't really God — just a poor imitation, like so many others in Hollywood vying for the position. Many people believe God up and left years ago, having been all but forced out of town. *Maybe He moved*, they think.

But I know He hasn't left. I know He loves stories, and even more, the people who tell them. I know this because I saw Him, the whole time. I saw Him in the dark places and the bright lights. He was with me in the lonely moments and at the big events. He wasn't always loud — usually He spoke in a still, small voice. But still, He was and is there, in Hollywood, hoping that maybe someone, anyone, might notice and listen to Him, the Creator of stories, so He can show us how to tell a better one.

In the coming pages, I will ask you to join me as I walk through the stories I gathered from my time as a struggling actor in Hollywood and discover how God was present in all of them. I will ask you to look with me at the power this world of story has and why each of us were made to live inside a good one. I will ask you to see that even though this place has lost its way, God is most assuredly still in La La Land.

Chapter 1

A Cross & The
Hollywood Sign

*"I live right under the Hollywood sign, so that
every day when I drive home, I'm reminded of why
I'm here."*
- Alessandro Nivola

If you drive up Highland Avenue, heading away from downtown Hollywood and into the jagged hills that surround her and look up, you'll see an interesting sight. On the cliffs overlooking the sparkling city, there are two unmissable monuments.

In the distance, to your right, you'll see The Hollywood Sign standing atop a mountain, surveying the endless expanse of Los Angeles. The Hollywood

Sign is something most of us have become all too familiar with as it has flashed across our screens, postcards, and minds for almost one hundred years, existing as a symbol for this crazy place and all the hopes of the millions that have flocked here for decades, following dreams and hoping to become stars. Even more than that, The Hollywood Sign serves as the mascot of the place where the stories of our time, and times past, are told, and the stories that have yet to be told will be brought to life. For some, The Hollywood Sign is one of hope, an answer to all the dreams that could be. But for others, it's a curse that represents a destructive influence that corrupts hearts and minds around the world.

If you look up and to your left, you'll see another symbol, an even older (and perhaps an even more controversial) one — a symbol with a story spanning back to the beginning of recorded time: a cross, a symbol very few don't have a connection or reaction to. The cross was originally designed as an instrument of death, but for the past two thousand years, because of one man, it has been seen as a visceral symbol of life to billions around the world, in almost every culture, country, and era since its appearance.

Each of these symbols are illuminated by lights at their base, shining up and bouncing off the white metal they are made of. Both are instantly recognizable around the world, each standing for something both meaningful and controversial, each symbolizing something powerful to countless people. But while they share much in common, they are entirely different.

~

I remember driving into Hollywood for the first time when I was only seventeen years old, the larger-than-life movie billboards and star-covered sidewalks passing by in the car window. I was taken by the mystique of this place, the place where the movies that had ignited my young imagination had been made. I was inexplicably drawn to the city. I knew, after five minutes of being within Los Angeles' city limits, that this would be the place where I chased my dreams.

I've always loved stories, since I was young –
beginning with my captivation with The Nest Bible
Cartoons. After watching, I would act out the stories I
had just witnessed with my willing family in our living
room. I always insisted on being the hero, and am still
famous in my family for dressing up as King David,
my performance being directed by my mother. In
response to my father, playing the role of Goliath,
asking me, "Are you a coward?" I bravely proclaimed,
"Yes, I am!"

When I was a bit older, I found myself taken with Old
Western and war movies, my favorite being *To Hell
and Back*, starring Audie Murphy, who was a
soldier-turned-actor who acted out his own inspiring
story of fighting through WWII on screen. I went to
the costume store where I found a helmet and a pair of
military boots to dress up like him for a school report.
After that, I decided I wanted to be an actor.

As a teenager, I found myself immersed in books like
The Lord of the Rings and *The Chronicles of Narnia*,
movies like *The Dark Knight* and *The Matrix*,

videogames like *Skyrim* and *The Legend of Zelda*, and music videos like "Welcome to the Black Parade," all of which ignited my imagination and heart. To me, movies, books, shows, games, and songs weren't just things to enjoy and drop; instead, they were all-consuming narratives that gave me a passion for life and the desire to discover the kind of story I wanted to tell with mine. I would pray that perhaps God would let me tell stories with my life, stories that would serve to help, inspire, and give the world hope. Stories where I could be a hero that would point a lost and hurting world back to their Creator.

So, when I was eighteen and it came time to decide what to do with my life, there was no question in my heart: I was going to be an actor. I can only imagine the fear and anxiety that must have shot through my parents' heads when I told them I'd be skipping college and going to acting school in New York City instead. But somehow, they trusted God and the dream He had placed on my heart. So with prayer and support, they wished me godspeed and sent me on my way.

Since I moved to Hollywood over a decade ago, I have gotten advice, received messages, and read articles, stating that Hollywood is not compatible with God. Likewise, I often hear on set, in class, or in meetings with managers, that God is not compatible with Hollywood. I will have to respectfully disagree with both of these sentiments.

If there's one thing that both The Hollywood Sign and The Hollywood Cross have in common it's this: they are both testaments to the power of stories. I believe stories are powerful; they have the ability to change, inspire, touch, and shape us in a way that nothing else can. Jesus changed the entire course of history (literally) through a ministry that consisted of him walking the dusty roads of his hometown telling... stories. Stories change us; stories change the world. It's hardwired that way into the very design of our humanity.

Through the ages, we have told our stories in different ways. Once upon a time, we painted pictures on cave walls with dyes from berries and blood. Then, we started telling our stories with words in dark huts lit only by fire, being passed down from generation to generation, from the old to the young, over and over again, until they became myth and legend. Then, we began to write them down on rocks, planks, and paper, spreading them far and wide, with a reach never before possible. Then, we wrote them into songs and on stages for them to come to life upon. Then, somehow, in just the past hundred years, we have arrived here, telling stories in a brand new way — but one that still echoes back to humanity's origins: film.

Film is a beautiful medium that combines so many of the artistic mediums (all, some would say), where visuals, music, audio, and performance are all combined into one piece of art to more fully and effectively tell our stories. Film is the way we tell our stories today.
So what better way to share God's love and truth with the world than through the most far-reaching and powerful art form mankind has ever seen?

~

Tonight, as I sit in my apartment in Hollywood, looking out the window, I can see just glimpses of The Hollywood Sign and The Cross. As I sit here, gazing into the dim night sky lit by hazy city lights and a roof of smog, I think back over the ten years of pursuing the dream God placed on my heart, and how each of these symbols have come to mean more to me than I ever knew they could. Both symbolize the thing I continue dedicating my life to. And both symbolize the thing I want to be a part of: stories.

So in the coming pages, I would love for you to join me on the journey that brought me here: all the ups and downs, the victories and disappointments, and the hopes and dreams I have experienced in my time finding God in Hollywood.

Chapter 2

All the World's a Stage

"People have forgotten how to tell a story. Stories don't have a middle or an end any more. They usually have a beginning that never stops beginning."
- Steven Spielberg

I was nineteen when I first stepped onto a real-life TV set. At the time, I was in acting school, learning the ins and outs of how to act, how to navigate the business, and how to breakdown a script. But in my off-time, late at night, lit only by the light of my computer screen, I quietly but eagerly submitted my headshot for roles on TV shows and films – which is how I nabbed my first appearance in a TV show as a background extra.

A couple of days before the shoot, I had gotten fitted for my outfit with the other actors, and by the time the actual day had arrived to shoot my scene, I felt ready for my big break.

All the afternoons spent playing pretend as a kid, all the evenings spent watching countless movies, and the late-night moments spent lying awake in my bed, imagining myself on the silver screen seemed to lead up to this moment. I remember my nervous energy and ever-present butterflies as I was shuttled to set, taking in everything happening around me. I watched as the crew and other actors prepared for a scene, and I couldn't help but feel like I was exactly where I was supposed to be.

It was a flashback scene and I was playing a soldier. I had been garbed in a 1970's military getup, complete from head-to-toe with body armor and a real rifle (with the motor taken out) while receiving stern looks from the propmaster. The other three soldiers and I were stuffed into a real armored vehicle, where we were to wait for our cue from the Assistant Director.

At that moment, I couldn't help but think back on all the times I had pretended to be a soldier as a kid with my friends in our backyards. I remember holding my breath as I waited for the scene to begin, nervous but excited. I felt my surroundings and attire and the sights and smells all causing me to lose myself and sink into this character, small as it may be, that I was chosen to play.

Then suddenly, for the first time in my life, I heard the Director yell, "Action!" And like a stage performer bursting from behind the curtain, I climbed out of the back of the car, gun blazing, teeth gritted, the sun above me acting as my very first spotlight as I played my part.

~

William Shakespeare once famously wrote...
"All the world's a stage,
And all the men and women merely players;
They have their exits and their entrances;
And one man in his time plays many parts."

His words articulate the idea that this world and everything in it is part of one big story, and that you and I are characters in this story. We each have a part to play that no one else can. We each have a calling and an arc; a beginning, middle, and end. Each of us are uniquely cast in this movie, play, or tale called life. Perhaps to most of us, this is just a nice sentiment. Maybe to others, it's a pile of silly nonsense. But in the passing years of my life, I keep on asking myself: what if it's true? What if we aren't just a random collection of atoms, floating in a sea of nothingness, headed for oblivion? What if, perhaps, our lives have meaning and we are a part of a greater narrative, and each of us, with every choice we make, are choosing the part we will play?

Well, if you will indulge me and entertain the belief for just a minute that you are a character in a truly epic and eternal story, and what you do matters, perhaps you, like me, are both excited and scared at the same time. Because if this is the case, if this is true, it means that life has indefinite meaning, our relationships are eternal, and our choices matter. Which is beautiful, but scary. It comes with the impetus to live lives of worth. When we allow ourselves to look at the world through the lens of story, we see ourselves and others in an entirely new and meaningful way. But there's another realization and set of questions that come with this belief: if this life is a story and has meaning, who set it in motion to begin with? Who is the creator, author, and director of this tale? It is here we must begin. To truly understand the story we are in, to truly live into the characters we were made to be, we must know the creator of the story.

Many of us shy away from the idea of believing this life has purpose. In my experience, it's often because of the implications that if we accept there's a director to the movie of life, it means that there is a right and a wrong way to live; that there is a script we can choose to follow, and there are directions we can decide to obey. Today, that simply is not a popular thing to believe. I sympathize with the fear, and sometimes wish I could do whatever I want without the reality of eternal consequence. But what I want even more is for my life to have beautiful purpose, which leads me to the desire to conform my life to the character I was made to play. And the only way I know how to do this effectively is to be in active communication with the One who has context on not just my life, but all of history. Who can see what I cannot, and I should listen to to help me live the role I was created to play. It's scary, frustrating, and humbling, but ultimately freeing.

~

Fresh out of high school, I carried big dreams of being a movie star in my heart, but my body was stuck in a little town in Colorado. I knew I had some natural talent — I was told so when people watched my homemade short films and local performances — but I knew I'd never fully realize my dreams until I got some training. I needed a director, a coach, someone who could look at me with objectivity and insight and help me hone and discover my art. So after a few late-night internet searches, I found an acting school in New York City and applied. My parents were cautiously supportive, encouraging me to follow the dream God had placed on my heart, even if it meant skipping college and any hope of a job with a consistent paycheck. Months later, I found myself in New York, studying acting, readying myself for the rest of my life.

It was a magical time. Everything seemed so fresh and new. All I had was the future, and it looked bright. I was put in a class with ten other students who became my makeshift family in a big city where I ventured out on my own for the first time. Together, we went to class daily, spending any time off reading through scenes and scripts together, preparing monologues, and doing acting exercises. Every couple of weeks, we were paired up with another student to study and memorize a scene, and then perform it for our class and teacher.

To this day, I still get nervous before I perform in front of a live audience, be it one filled with thousands of people, or even worse, a handful of your closest friends. But after taking a few deep breaths as I stood right outside of the small blackbox theater where we held class, I was excited for the chance to yet again play pretend, and live out whatever story I had been assigned. We performed on a small stage covered with simple props, a couch, a bed, a table, and a lamp, all to create the illusion of reality in our scenes. And just feet beyond the stage, beneath the dimmed lights, sat James, our teacher, notepad in hand, ready to observe our scene.

James was a mysterious man, filled with passion for acting as well as sharp insight into people and the human condition. He himself was a student of the renowned acting teacher Sanford Meisner, and had become one of the most respected acting coaches in New York. James had an uncanny ability to draw authentic human performances out of his actors in ways others could not. While often being unsettlingly blunt, he was always honest, with the intention to draw you and the story you were telling to its best.

The group would go quiet, the lights would dim, and the stage would sit, waiting for us to arrive. My partner and I would stand offstage, taking deep breaths, praying to remember the lines, and hoping to give our best performance. We would enter and the scene would start, each of us speaking the lines we'd been given. We would read each other and try to remain in the moment, putting to work all the skills we had gained over the months of training. And then, finally the last line would be said. We would take one last beat, then one of us would say, "Scene," signifying that the scene had come to an end. Then each of us would approach James' desk, pull up a chair, and wait for his notes. James would have his legs crossed, his brows furrowed, thinking deeply as he tapped his fingers on his table.

Then he would go through his notes, telling each actor his perspective on how the scene might improve. Sometimes he would ask questions, sometimes he would make definitive statements, and other times he would outright call you out. But no matter his comments, they always came out of a place of trying to help us give the best performance we could. It was humbling, sitting in front of James. It's scary performing in front of someone with so much knowledge, experience, and insight. But after watching myself grow stronger as an actor, I learned it's worth pushing through the fear.

I wonder if that is how we ought to be with God. If perhaps, God is watching us perform with a perspective of wisdom and love, one that comes from a desire for us to live the best story we can and act out the stories we were made to tell. If this is true, the only way it's possible is to humble ourselves enough to go and sit at His desk and listen to God's notes, which He has conveniently already written down in a book you might have heard of.

~

I have worked with directors before who believed that getting the best performance out of their actors came through yelling, anger, or even threats. I've watched as young actors were left embarrassed and broken under an authoritarian director who used shame as a method to produce the performance they wanted. I have also worked with directors before who simply said nothing, expecting their cast to figure it all out of their own. The actors would grasp at straws and stumble around in the dark, spending the entire scene trying to guess what the director wanted, having been provided no guidance. And lastly, I have worked with hands-on, caring, communicative directors; directors who took the time to connect with the actor, express their vision, and guide them to a better scene that ultimately made a better story and a better movie.

I think many of us view God either as an angry authority, or a passive, uncaring, distant observer. Both of these pictures of God are ones I think few of us would want to work with, much less give our trust to in building our stories. Why would we? On one hand, we live in fear, worrying that we will mess up, and then bear the weight of shame when we do. On the other, we are anxiously trying to do our best, but ultimately are lost, having no direction or communication.

But what if, to our surprise, we realized that God isn't disappointed or angry, and God isn't indifferent or distant, either? How would it change our performance in our lives and our stories to have the realization that God is loving and caring, active and communicative? What if we understood that God wants to help us rise to the best performance He knows we can live — not for His own sake, but for ours? Like James, my acting teacher, God does this through insightfully sharing His perspective that comes from a place of wisdom and care for you and the story you're telling, a perspective that you cannot see on your own, a perspective He offers astutely enough to not break your spirit, but strongly enough to build it.

~

God wants us to take part in the story He is, and has been, telling since the dawn of humanity. But like any skilled director, He has set the film in motion and called us each to live out the unique roles that he has created us to. He does not force us to play the part He wrote for us, but should we go to Him, talk to Him, and listen to Him, we might just find wisdom, insight, and loving guidance into how we can better play the role He has created us to live.

Chapter 3

Makeup & Masks

"Acting is different than stand-up. It gives you the
ability to enter into another character. To create
another person."
- Robin Williams

It was late — really late. Midnight had come and gone
an hour ago, but we were all still on set, buried in a
soundstage somewhere deep inside the walls of one of
the big studios in the center of Los Angeles. As a new
kid in Hollywood looking to find my "big break" and
still wanting to pay rent, I had continued my career as
a background artist, having trudged down to Central
Casting early one morning, signing up to be a
full-time movie and TV extra. After a while, I fell into
a regular gig of playing a student on the popular new
high school musical-drama, *Glee*.

It wasn't as glamorous as I made it sound to people back home. It mostly consisted of being ordered around by the tired Production Assistants, and then standing and sitting around for sometimes fifteen hours a day, all for just $8 an hour and a bag of chips. But at least I was on set, getting to be a part – albeit a small one – of the stories being told, taking one more step towards reaching the dream in my heart. In my head, I had visions of being the *star*, daydreams of landing the leads in movies seen by millions. But for now, I would have to be content being a blur in the background.

It was cold inside the enormous soundstage, but there was still an exciting buzz in the air as the crew garbed in cargo pants and black t-shirts shuffled back and forth, setting up the next shot while the Director stood by the camera, looking across the set, planning the next scene.

I stood, caked with makeup and dressed in a letterman jacket (I played one of the jocks), next to a handful of other extras, each representing the high school stereotypes. We fidgeted on our starting marks, interjecting whispered off-hand comments to make each other smile as we all looked on, waiting for our cues. After everything had found its place and the next shot was ready to go, someone called out, "First team!" signaling the *star actors'* arrival on set.

All of a sudden, there he was — the star of the whole show, Cory. He was strikingly handsome, tall. His presence commanded attention as he entered the room. I had seen him everywhere recently: on magazine covers in checkout lines, on billboards staring at me while I drove down Sunset Boulevard, and on the old TV set I shared with the three other struggling actors I rented an apartment with. But now, here he was in front of me, in the flesh, and all I could think was how the pictures didn't do him justice.

As he walked to his mark, ready to begin, all eyes were on him, including mine. Suddenly, I found myself wishing to be where he was, to do what he did, to have what he had. He possessed good-looks and talent, he was the leading man on a hit TV show, and was even dating the beautiful lead actress. From where I was standing, both literally and figuratively, he had it all.

Someone yelled, "Action!" and the scene began. With passion and nuance, he delivered his lines, sang his song, and hit his marks. Meanwhile, I (somewhat less importantly) did my crosses behind him when I was signaled, but as soon as I was off-camera, I would turn to capture a glimpse of him in action. I was so close, but so far. I couldn't help but want what he had.

There are no small parts, there are no small parts, there are no small parts, I breathed to myself silently, trying to make myself feel better, knowing I was little more than a blur in the background. But as I watched Cory effortlessly come to life in front of the camera, I found myself starstruck.

Someone yelled, "Cut!" and the scene ended. Cory disappeared into the lights of the studio, back to his trailer, and into the charmed life I could only fantasize about. But even as he vanished from sight, his image had been seared in my mind, suddenly becoming the picture of everything I longed for.

Years passed as I kept his image alive in my mind, letting him embody everything I thought I wanted. Until one fateful morning, I woke up to my computer screen sharing the terrible news that Cory had been found dead in his hotel room after overdosing, ultimately ending his own life.

I laid back in bed, letting my gaze drift to the ceiling. I hadn't known the young actor on any level deeper than sharing a smile as we would pass one another in the studio halls, or while grabbing a snack at craft services ("crafty"). But for some reason, the news of his passing hit me like a punch to the gut.

I did my best to make sense of the troubling headlines, but still, I was left empty.

How could this have happened? For so long, his bright image and magnetic smile in magazines, across TV, and even in person that night two years before had served as a picture of the perfect life I wanted. But now, that image had been shattered by the reality that all along, right beneath the surface of the bright face I thought I wanted, there had been a darkness hiding that no one could see. I worked only a couple more times on the show after his passing. But the light had gone out of that place, the magic had faded, and I can't help but wonder if it was ever there to begin with.

~

I've always loved getting my makeup done for shoots. I enjoy sitting in "the chair," staring at my face and watching in real time as the blemishes, scars, and imperfections disappear, as the makeup artist does their work. Of course they're still there, hiding just beneath the surface, but no one can tell.

I grew up the youngest son and third child of a pastor and a popular Christian author and speaker. Growing up was a whirlwind of traveling around the country, and even the world, as my family's ministry grew larger and larger. We would spend months out of the year putting on conferences for thousands of people looking to my family to see what a good Christian family should be, and what good Christian kids should look like.

Part of me loved the attention and wanted to take on that image that everyone saw on stage and read stories about in books and blog posts... but another part was fighting battles no one but me and God could see. No one could see the doubts, depression, and demons I was fighting beneath the surface of an expected smile. Most couldn't see the OCD breakdowns, the medication I took for my messed-up brain, my bubbling anger, and despairing thoughts.

Even now, in my 30s, when asked, "How are you, Nathan?" my immediate reaction is to reply with an exuberant, "Great!" detailing all the success I'm having in life, all the while wearing a smile you could see your face in.

But if you were to peel back the thin layer of makeup I cover myself with, you just might find the *real* me — covered with the blemishes of crippling mental illness, the scars of incessant insecurity, and the warts of sadness, doubt, and comparison that I hope no one sees.

~

It's such a human tendency to create masks to cover the broken parts of our stories, protecting ourselves from the world ever seeing us for what we really are... *human*.

All of us have fractured places in our lives, hiding just beneath the surface, and no matter how beautiful of a mask we create, we have darkness in us that simply won't go away, no matter how carefully a disguise is made.

Our masks might look different, some taking the form of a movie star, while others are woven together to give the appearance of a "good" Christian kid. And we might wear these masks for different reasons – for some of us, maybe it's the insecurity of not looking "good enough," for others, it's the fear of disappointing the ones around us, and for many of us, we are simply scared we are not enough, so we wear a mask hoping to convince the world around us that we are.

But no matter what our reasons, we all wear them –
using them to hide who we are behind our perfectly
constructed Facebook profiles, impressive resumes,
and expensive clothes, hoping to keep the darker parts
of ourselves hidden from the world around us.

And the thing is, for a while, it works. We find
ourselves able to play the part, read the lines, and put
on the show, keeping our darkness from falling and
seeping through the cracks, into the painful light. But
eventually, no matter how hard we try, the makeup
will smudge and the mask will break, forcing us to
come face to face with who we really are.

I believe it's at this point that we have a choice: to let
the reality of our brokenness consume us and drive us
to despair and destruction, or to let it lead us to God,
the One who created us, loves us unconditionally, and
wants to begin the process of not just covering up the
brokenness but instead, putting the pieces of us back
together.

Sometimes I wish I had taken the chance I had that
one night to let Cory know that despite the demons

he was facing, hiding just beneath the facade of a perfect movie star, that there was hope for light in the midst of his darkness. And while I can't tell him, I can tell you.

So, go to your Creator and find healing, peace, acceptance, and love. You need only take off your mask.

Chapter 4

Heaven & The Golden Age
of Hollywood

*"My son tells me, 'Do you realize you are the last
one? The last person who was an eyewitness to the
golden age?' Young people, even in Hollywood, ask
me, 'Were you really married to Humphrey
Bogart?' 'Well, yes, I think I was,' I reply. You
realize yourself when you start reflecting – because
I don't live in the past, although your past is so
much a part of what you are – that you can't
ignore it."*

- Lauren Bacall

If you walk down Hollywood Boulevard and look
down, there, next to the littered streets and on dirty
sidewalks beneath your feet you'll find bronze stars
cemented into the walkway. The walkway covered in

stars stretches on for miles, and across each star is a name, many of whom harken back to a different time in Hollywood: The Golden Age.

The Golden Age of Hollywood was a time that lives in a permanent and potent nostalgia, lit by shimmering lights and classic glitz. It was the period when movies had newly burst forth into the world as the most magical and powerfully artistic storytelling medium the universe had ever seen. Its players were grand and demigod-like, garbed in three-piece suits and silk gowns. They spoke with Transatlantic accents and danced across movie theater screens with elegant style, telling not the gritty human stories we tell today, but instead, showing us a world that was better than humanity, causing all who gazed upon the spectacle to long to be swept up in its alluring shine. This age is an age shrouded in sparkling mystery, beckoning us back to a time of classy parties, red carpets, pithy dialogue, and a polished reality that stands in stark contrast to the messiness of our own reality.

As a kid, I would watch the TCM channel with my mom, looking on as the actors dressed in black and white spun enchanting tales of love, mystery, and adventure. I watched Audrey Hepburn in *Charade*, Cary Grant in *North by Northwest*, Debbie Reynolds in *Singin' in the Rain*, and Jimmy Stewart in *It's a Wonderful Life*.

I fell into the inviting stories as a boy and longed to live inside them. But even beyond just the screen, I felt a pull to the place and magic of a Hollywood era that seemed frozen in time, or maybe from an alternate universe – one many idealize and long for, even now. We long for it because it showed us not what reality is, but what it *could* be. It showed us romance, order, and beauty, each an aspect that every human heart longs for, but it showed us these things in a way that, unlike real life, was beautiful and good.

The Golden Age of Hollywood has been explored in modern TV shows, like Ryan Murphy's *Hollywood*, films like the Coen brothers' *Hail, Caesar!*, and even video games like *L.A. Noire*. These works lift the idealistic veil and show the darker side of the world we have nostalgically misunderstood, which in truth, was filled with addiction, abuse, despair, and sadness

— just like the world we're currently living in. But still, we seem obsessed with this era and indescribably drawn to its enticing alternate universe, one that shows us not how the world actually is, but perhaps, as it *should* be. The stories that Hollywood wove tapped into our intrinsic human desire for a utopia.

At the same time as the Golden Age of Hollywood, another movement came to prominence in America: Christian Fundamentalism — which stood in stark contrast to everything Hollywood displayed. If Hollywood was flashy and dramatic, they would be still and tepid. If Hollywood wooed people with great stories of romance and adventure, they would warn people about the evils of sex.

The Fundamentalists were a new form of Puritans who thought all the things and beauty of the world were evil, perhaps forgetting that it was God who had made the world beautiful. With a reactionary mindset, they began the systematic process of removing anything that looked like it might ignite the senses and could lead people into sin and out of the safe walls of the church. They were obsessed with modesty, temperance, and moralism, to the point where dancing and collar bones were quickly considered sinful "stumbling blocks," never thinking that perhaps pride and judgmentalism could be as well.

I imagine it was with good intentions that they waged their war on culture, hoping to address and eradicate the destructive ways of the world — but in their fear, they threw the beautiful out with the bathwater. The church that used to live inside of glorious cathedrals, patronize the greatest artists in the world, and write soaring music inspired from a living God was trading its beauty for white-washed walls and a theology of fear and shame.

As I look at the origin stories of these two groups, both vying for the world's attention, it's little wonder to me why "Godless" Hollywood won. Of course, there is darkness beneath the shining lights of Hollywood, but on the surface, it's a celebration of beauty, adventure, passion, purpose, and great stories — things God has placed on our souls to long for. And instead of redeeming and saving the created beauty of

God from the clutches of a selfish world, the church eradicated God's beauty out of fear. Both the church and Hollywood showed us what the world *could* be, and between the visions they cast, the people chose the one that more fully resonated with the deepest desires of the human heart, not the one that shamed them for their God-given longings. Which is why today, the church is sadly seen as an irrelevant and outdated institution. Even with all its darkness, Hollywood continues to woo the world into its enticing promises, because it offers what the church no longer does: wonder, beauty, acceptance, and purpose.

~

I fell in love with God early in my life. I fell in love with Him because I was shown a God who is big and beautiful; a God who loves adventure, dancing, mystery, music, and collar bones; a God who came to earth and told stories, laughed with children, and gave grace, love, and purpose to the downtrodden and forgotten – that is the kind of God that can compete with the glamor of Hollywood, not one stripped of everything beautiful and covered over with white-washed walls, monotone hymns, and unreachable moral lists.

When God created the world, He said it was good. He proclaimed goodness over dancing, music, adventure, sex, food, skin, breasts, laughter, colors, and everything other thing that our hearts desire. But the world took these wonderful things and, with selfish hands, corrupted them. We see this exemplified daily in places like Hollywood. But the way to join in the work of redeeming the world isn't by getting rid of them — instead, we must more fully live into the beauty He has created us to desire, to go to the heart of our desires, where we will find God in all of His joyful glory and learn how exactly these gifts were made to be engaged with.

I remember once working as a staff member at a film premiere in Los Angeles for a movie starring Brad Pitt. It was being held in the heart of Hollywood at one of its oldest and most famous theaters. After all the celebrities and important people had stepped off the red carpet and into the screening, me and a couple of the other staffers snuck inside the old theater. The interior was draped with red velvet and painted with gold; there were glass cases with relics, props, and costumes from old classic movies; it was covered with intricately carved, arched ceilings, encapsulating a place that inspired wonder and joy.

I was overtaken with a feeling that reminds me of another time, when I stepped into a cathedral in New York City and was immediately confronted with the majestic beauty of elaborate stained glass, artistic molded figures, and soaring gothic ceilings that, again, inspired something deep inside of me to respond to the beauty I was being confronted with — beauty that was inspired by and made for a big and beautiful God.

~

God is every bit as glamorous, exciting, adventurous, and mysterious as Hollywood. What flashing light in La La Land could hold a candle to the ever-expanding, glimmering galaxies that are stretched out across the sky for all the world to see? We were created to desire a wonderful world, like the alluring and captivating

ones we imagine when we think of old Hollywood —
why do you think John describes heaven as having
streets of gold? Our desire for beauty is a good thing,
but too often, God's followers have tried to hide the
beauty He has created in our world out of fear. May
we be people who don't run from beauty, but seek to
live inside, redeem, and use it, so that it may call all
who encounter it to a more beautiful life with their
Creator.

Chapter 5

The Audition

"When I was younger, I would go to auditions to have the opportunity to audition, which would mean another chance to get up there and try out my stuff, or try out what I learned and see how it worked with an audience, because where are you gonna get an audience?"
- Al Pacino

I nervously walked into a small waiting room lit by an unflattering fluorescent light. A woman at a small desk motioned me over to sign in. I wrote down my name, contact number, and the role I was auditioning for. I set the pen down and walked to an empty chair in the corner, where I could better survey the room. Around me sat six other actors. They all looked like slightly different versions of me, one taller Nathan, one fitter Nathan, one handsomer Nathan, and one shorter Nathan. I looked down at the headshot in my hands. Staring back at me was a picture of my face, or something that resembled it, but with less lines and blemishes, with more controlled hair than the non-cooperating 'do I was sporting today. On the back of my headshot was my resume – not as long as I'd like it to be – filled with embellished credits, hoping the casting director would be impressed, or at least less disappointed. I glanced over at the headshot and resume of the guy next to me, handsome Nathan; his picture looked better, and as he turned his page over, I could see his resume was longer. Shoot.

I recollected myself, took a breath, and gave taming my wild hair one more go. The audition was for a popular TV show. In my heart, I wanted to believe that this could be my moment, this could be the thing that would finally break me out of obscurity and into my dream. But in my head, I held little hope I could do it. After a couple of years and hundreds of auditions, very few had materialized into much at all. It was easier not to get my hopes up, but I couldn't stop the nagging desire to dream.

Suddenly, the door to the audition room opened. I heard friendly laughter from voices inside as Tall Nathan walked out.

"Nathan Clarkson?" the woman at the desk called out.

"That's me," I replied. I stood up, took a deep breath, and headed into the room.

I walked in to see three people sitting behind a thick table. None of them looked up. They kept their eyes on their phones and pads. I set my headshot on the table and one of them grabbed it, took a cursory glance at the picture, looked up at me, then flipped it over and looked at my resume for what seemed about 1.3 seconds before tossing it back on the table.

"When you're ready."

I felt my palms begin to sweat as I took one quick glance at the small camera recording what I hoped would be genius, but feared would be failure, before I launched into my short scene. It was neither – it was just okay. I gave my lines, perhaps a bit shakier than I had practiced them in the mirror at home. I did my actions, though a little more stilted than I had imagined them in my head, and I finished.

I waited. One of them gave a flat grin and said, "Thanks," and that was it. I walked out.

I didn't get the part. Maybe because I didn't do the best I could. But sometimes I wonder if I would've, had I not carried both the weight of my dreams and the desperation for them to like me into the room with me. I also wonder how much better I would've performed had they curated a warmer place in which to perform. But either way, that was not my big break.

~

The first audition I ever booked was after I had woken up at a friend's house. I was unshowered, tired, sporting dark undereye circles, bedhead, and wearing a wrinkled white T-shirt. Up to that point, before every audition I attended, I would take an hour to get ready, comb, shave, wash up, and wear only my nicest-looking clothes. So when I got the call to go to a last-minute audition, I thought, *Well, I'm a mess, but I guess I'll go anyway.* During the audition, I actually broke into laughter multiple times and asked to start over (a big no-no). Walking out, I was sure there was no possible way I'd hear from them again. How could I? I was a *mess*. But lo and behold, a few days later, I got the call that I had been cast.

My friend Adrian and I became friends after attending five of the same auditions, for the same roles, and neither of us booked any of them. We eventually decided, after trying to crack the audition code, that there was something to not worrying about it and embracing the mess going to auditions. We figured out that when we were more authentic, real, less polished, and even messy, the casting directors seemed to react more positively.

~

For years, I carried with me the same fear, nervousness, and anxiety I had going to auditions as I did going to God. I felt it necessary to clean up, put on my best clothes, and fix my appearance before going to Him. I found myself setting my resume of good works in front of Him, hoping that would manipulate me into His favor. And I always left feeling that no matter how hard I tried, I had failed, and God would cast the next guy in the role of who He gave His love and affection to.

But through the years of going to God, just like with my auditions, I began finding that the more honest I was with God, the more okay I became simply talking to Him instead of performing for Him; the more comfortable appearing like the mess I truly was in front of Him, the closer I felt to Him. I found that God isn't holding auditions for His love. I've already been cast as His child, who he would and *did* die for.

God loves me not as a casting director waiting for me to mess up, but as a parent who is rooting for my best. I realized all the time I spent trying to airbrush my photos and impress him was wasted. He simply loves me. I already have the part.

~

My first reaction when on camera, be it on set or taking a selfie, is to adjust myself — my posture, face, and body — to be as attractive as I can be; to angle myself so I will be seen only in a becoming light. But the problem is, when acting in a deeply human, dramatic, or meaningful scene, the point is not to look good, but rather perform in an honest way that will connect with the viewer. Trying to look good when filming a dramatic scene will only make you look stilted, stiff, and cold. It's only in releasing the fear of how you will look that you are free enough to perform in a way that will be impactful. The greatest, most meaningful moments in movies I have watched are the scenes where the actors themselves look the worst. With their face askew, hair in their eyes, and bodies hunched or sprawled. Oftentimes, the actor is covered in tears, snot, or mud, and their voices crack and whine. But in their letting go, they find something beautiful to offer the scene, and ultimately, the viewer.

~

It's natural for humans to want to earn and prove and work for acceptance, both from the world and from God. But perhaps when we learn to be more comfortable with the messy parts of who we are — the unshowered, unpressed parts – we will find more freedom both in our life around us and in our relationship with God.

You need not audition for God's love. You have already been cast as His child.

Chapter 6

More, Please

"In my mind, I've always been an A-list Hollywood
superstar. Y'all just didn't know yet."
- Will Smith

For years, I idealized getting a "line" — just one line,
heck, one *word* in a TV show. I had spent so many
days, hours, and months walking as a blur in the
background. To imagine myself getting to have the
camera on me, to be important enough to actually be
part of a scene in some sort of meaningful way,
became an obsession. I dreamt about it, I wanted it, I
prayed for it. Getting a line is somewhat of an actor's
badge of honor, signifying that you are a "real" actor
and not just a wannabe. And I wanted so badly to not
just be a wannabe.

Then, one day, I finally got what I had wanted for so long. I got my first featured role on a TV show. I had one line – well, one *word*, actually. But the casting director on the phone said I had been "picture picked" by the director himself. It was a new (but now beloved) show, and I could feel my heart leap as she shared the news I had waited so long to get. Hanging up my phone, I was unsure if it was a prank or if I was imagining it. For so long, my time on screen had been spent in obscurity. But now, I got to be in focus – front and center, in a real scene, a scene where I mattered.

There were shots of excitement and twinges of nervousness as I wove my way through Los Angeles, toward the filming location. I got to the studio early, giving myself just a few minutes to catch my breath and enjoy the moment I had pictured in my head for the last decade.

Minutes later, I found myself I wandering through the maze of trailers and people rushing to and fro, eventually finding an out of breath Production Assistant who ushered me in and through wardrobe, hair, and makeup. I had just enough time to stand in the breakfast line and talk to the then-young star of the show, Donald. He was nice, laughed at my joke, and made one of his own. Donald is now a famous movie star. But then, he was just starting out. Donald was in my scene – or I should say, I was in Donald's. I played the titular role of "Surprised Student" in a scene that took place in a pretend classroom, made with three fake walls that left room for the large camera, lights, and twenty crew members looking on.

The director gave me my instructions: to notice Donald passing by the window doing something crazy, then turn to another classmate and say, "Look," – not exactly the meaty Oscar-worthy role I had dreamed of, but that day, to me, it was the most important role in Hollywood. I was on top of the world.

The entire five second scene took about an hour to shoot. Then, I was done. Was I a movie star now?

Driving home that night, I felt I had finally arrived. It might've been just one line (or *word*), but it was *my* line. I had taken my first real step on the journey of living my dreams. All those days of being a background actor were done. I was now a real actor.

The high of that day lasted for a good three days. Then it soon faded into a need for another hit. I'd had the first small taste of getting what I had always dreamed of, and instead of satiating the longing in my heart like I thought it would, it made me even more hungry than I had been before.

~

The movie *La La Land* revolves around two star-crossed lovers living the life of starving artists together in LA. With beautiful shots of beautiful people living in the City of Angels, each chasing the dream in their heart, we watch as dance numbers come to life on the streets, and musical interludes colorfully light up the backdrop of Hollywood. In the end, both characters achieve their dreams, but only after they give up on each other, a necessary choice these characters must make to find what they truly want – or so we are led to believe.

Walking out of the theater after watching it for the first time, my friends and the people around me were oohing and aahing over the visually dazzling movie, but deep in my gut I knew very little of what I had just watched was true.

On the screen, we saw a polished and colorful city, oozing a magical and irresistable aesthetic strong enough to make any young wide-eyed dreamer want to pack it all up and head to Hollywood. But from the years I had spent in that place, I knew better. I knew it was all a beautiful lie. The movie had used magic to hide the truth of what La La Land really is.

Los Angeles, in reality, is filled with endless miles of strip malls that are peppered with strip clubs, only broken up by wealthy gated communities, whose residents pretend those places don't exist. Los Angeles lives in a neverending sweaty temperature, burning beneath a bright sun, dulled by a thick layer of smog hanging over the countless streets covered in homeless people, constant traffic, garbage-lined sidewalks, and cheap apartments filled with naïvely hopeful people. People who, unlike the characters in the movie, never end up catching their dreams. Instead, they watch them die a slow death over the course of years, while this city keeps making promises it never planned to make good on.

~

Not too long ago, I attended a big primere right in the middle of Hollywood. There were flashing lights, pushing paparazzi, and about a million pretty people dressed to the nines, all excited for their turn to walk the red carpet. My more successful friend had invited me, and I gladly accepted the chance to feel important for a night. I wore my nicest pair of jeans, and to really dress things up, put a sport coat over my T-shirt.

For the first hour at the celebration after the movie, I tried to enjoy myself, grabbing an hors d'oeuvre or a glass of champagne when I could, smiling my brains out and trying to "network." But talking about pointless things, smiling, and inane conversation wears me out, so I decided to step outside for a breath of fresh air.

The air wasn't fresh; it was muggy and present, but it would have to do. Muffled sounds from the DJ's music and the sea of voices we cut to size as the door closed behind me. I took a breath in. Mid-breath, I heard voices. I looked over and saw a few people hanging out on the sidewalk, apparently having had the same idea. With a closer look, I realized the woman standing in between the two other men was the star actress of the film I had just seen. She was dressed in an expensive, long gown that now seemed to cause her grief, as it wouldn't quite stay up the way she wanted. She had a half-finished cocktail in her hand and was obviously drunk, leaning on walls and people to stay upright. She saw me and asked for a light for her cigarette. It was then that I looked in her eyes and saw what I have seen so many times in that town, on both the famous and the nobodies, on the rich and the poor: I saw sadness.

Maybe it was in my head. But on her big night, she was outside, almost unable to stand up. It made me wonder, what had Hollywood promised this woman? She was a famous actress now, but the sadness I saw in her eyes didn't seem to care who she was. The image of her face is painted in my mind as one of a lost little girl. She had found fame, money, and notoriety, so she had found everything she could want, right? I'm not so sure.

~

Each and every human was created with a desire for more. We were created with a deep longing for purpose, love, value, relationship, and meaning. This "want" can take us on a journey that draws us closer to God, or it can lead us to our own demise.

Hollywood, and the world in general, capitalizes on our human and intrinsic desire for these things we were made to want, and like a smooth talking salesman, offers us cheap imitations of what we were made for. La La Land lures the young, the innocent, and the vulnerable with promises of their heart's desires, and instead takes more than anyone knew they would pay.

All the things Hollywood and the world offer are just cheap imitations of what will truly salve and satisfy the human needs we each have. We're told that fame, money, and status will give us what we truly want. But no amount of any of these things will ever come close to being enough.

Chapter 7

The Cry

"Acting is behaving truthfully under imaginary
circumstances."

- **Sanford Meisner**

I was sitting down in the bathroom of a motel room
thirty miles outside of Los Angeles. Above me worked
a few crew members, setting up for the next shot, the
shot for the pivotal scene in a TV series I had been
cast in a month before. The scene scared me – not
because it involved dangerous stunts, not because I
had a long, difficult monologue, but because I had to
cry. For many, actors crying on cue is as easy as
laughing on cue. But for me, crying on command in
front of a room full of strangers, much less alone with
myself, was a terrifying feat. Not because I was
insecure about looking weak or vulnerable; I had
gotten over looking ridiculous in front of other people

at the ripe old age of three. It scared me because I didn't know how. Crying, displaying the outpouring of emotion, is something I've never been able to control. It's something that seems to strike me when it feels it wants, and eludes me when I want.

The light above me cast a beautiful warm light in the small room, setting the stage for the cinematic feel of the serious drama that was being created. It was hot and I felt beads of sweat race down my forehead.
"You ready?" the director, David, asked.
"Yes," I nodded nervously, not believing myself.
"Quiet on set!" the director yelled. A hush fell quickly over the previously bustling room. This was it – my time to shine.
"And... action."

I could feel all eyes on me as I tried, pointlessly, to shut out the world. I could feel a heat rise beneath my skin, partly from the lights above me and partly from the fear I couldn't shake. But I couldn't wait any longer. I put my head in my hands and pretended to cry. After a few moments, hoping the director got what he needed so we could move on I heard: "Cut."

I looked up, the director was looking at me resting his hand on his mouth thinking.

"I want to do it again," he said.

Great, I didn't get it, I thought to myself. I guess I'm not born to be a real actor, a one-take wonder actor.

"But Nathan..."

"Yes?"

"One tweak. Don't cover your face when you cry. I want to see that. That's where the emotion is."

"Okay," I said, knowing this time, there was no hiding. This time, I had to actually find a way to reach the edge of myself for the sake of this scene. If I didn't, I think I'd still be in that motel bathroom. I reached in my pocket, rubbed some menthol chapstick on my finger, and gently patted it beneath my eye – an old actor trick to produce tears. Hopefully, this would get the emotion engine running.

"Quiet on set!" the director yelled again, "And... action!"

Again, I could feel eyes all over me. I could feel the camera staring like a gun at my head. Everything in me wanted to raise my hands to cover my face, to hide the emotion, or lack thereof. But then, suddenly, as the menthol coerced some moisture from my eyes, as I sat there totally naked, unable to cover my face, I felt a real and true piece of emotion hit me. Tears fell as I had nowhere left to hide, and I leaned into the character and context of the story. It was almost as if through the very action of not covering my face, of not hiding, I was able to feel more fully and deeply what my character was going through and cry.

"Cut. Beautiful. We got it."

~

We've all seen this kind of scene, in some form or another, weaving itself through the most famous and beloved films of all time. As it seems to be a universal picture, I have to wonder what about it so connects and relates to us that we would, over and over again, portray it in the stories we tell.

There are moments in art when you see such passion, desperation, and utter abandon displayed, and it seems to echo something beyond the confining nature of this broken world.

~

I have a friend named Lou, who is also my talent
manager. I met Lou at my first acting teacher Rich's
apartment at a get together for artists of faith. After I
made a snide remark to something he said, we became
fast friends. Everyone should have a Lou in their life.
With Lou, I am allowed to be honest, to curse, to tell
him my lowest and darkest thoughts, to express my
anger, to use swear words and have him not flinch or
judge. Lou allows me to exercise my demons with him,
not censoring me, but allowing me to experience
catharsis through the expression of the angst inside
my heart.

Lou is a cultured man. He has fine tastes and possesses
an endless knowledge of movies, plays, classical music,
and art. Lou and I often go to the movies, see
Broadway plays, and attend art museums. One night,
Lou invited me to the opera. I had an appreciation
from afar, but it wasn't until I was sitting in the
Metropolitan Opera House, confronted with the
majestic sets, and rich music that I fully grasped what

it was. I can still remember being on the edge of my seat, experiencing something I had never seen before — but that somehow echoed to familiar places in my heart. From the second the performance began, I was put under a spell. The sopranos, tenors, and chorus sang with such passion, leaving nothing behind, letting the tragic story unfold, laying completely bare in their performances. It was truly beautiful.

A few nights later, at Lou's apartment, he asked me to share some of my music with him. Music is a regular and needed part of my day, like water or food. It feeds my soul, enabling me to carry on through the sometimes difficult moments of life. I listen to it on my long walks down city streets at night, or in cafes as I try to conjure up inspiration, and sometimes, I listen to it in the dark of my room, laying in bed, needing something to embody externally what I feel internally.

Since he had shown me opera, so filled with passion and desperation, I decided to show him the music of my youth, known to many as the aptly-named screamo: heavy rock music with vocals that could rip your shirt off. I listened to it as a teenager, and to be honest, still do when I'm having an especially difficult day. It still seems the only music that can quite capture the deeper emotions in my life, while offering relief, and ultimately, freedom. So I played it for Lou. I watched Lou's face as I pushed play, the heavy metal booming in his apartment through his surround-sound speakers. I was expecting a confused look and a condescending crack from the cultured artist. But he gave only interest. As the last of the slamming drums, thumping bass, and screaming vocals faded out, I sat, waiting for his review. He looked at me after a moment of pensive thought, admitting that it was different than what he was used to. But then he said understood it. He said, like opera, he could feel the passion and raw emotion the artist shared. Lou told me of a concept called The Cry, a longing in every human's heart that makes itself known in our desperation. Sometimes it comes out as a High C, other times, a scream.

But The Cry is something we are all familiar with. We see it in paintings, where the artist is able to capture the raw emotion of the human soul so clearly in the face of his subject. Or in dance, when the dancer is so moved by the music, every move she makes is made with such precise passion that it doesn't look human. Or in movies (my favorite), when the actor lets go of all his inhibitions, going to the edge of himself as he authentically portrays the depths of human emotion. But all of this simply visually illustrates the actual Cry that rests in each of our own hearts.

While it so often appears in paintings, music, and film, those are only representations inspired by The Cry in our actual hearts. They are the artistic reflections of the actual moments in our lives when we are pushed to the edge of our humanity, forcing us to look up and let out a "cry" to God. It can happen in the most beautiful moments in life and in the most broken. It might happen in a church pew, when you don't know if you believe anymore, or a cubicle in front of a cold, dead screen, when you don't know if you can carry on one more day. It could happen in a dark alley while fighting an addiction you've been wrestling for years, or maybe staring at an empty pantry when you have a family to feed, or it could be in an apartment in Los Angeles, where a relationship you thought would last forever falls apart.

~

I think everyone hears The Cry from inside us, but so often we try to ignore it, or as I did, cover our faces to hide it. We do this because we can't bear the feelings that draw us to such depths of ourselves that they make us come in close contact to the eternity we can't explain. So often we turn on Christian radio, and hope the positive words and upbeat major chords will drown out the deep longing at the broken places in our hearts. Sometimes, as a result of Hallmark-like Christian movies where everything works out in the end, upbeat Christian music that never delves too deep, and self-help Christian books that always have an easy fix, we can feel like "good" Christians aren't supposed to feel sad, and we are just supposed to be happy. And if we aren't happy, we're doing something wrong.

But if you look at the characters throughout Scripture who truly loved God, you find The Cry weaving itself through almost all of the stories of the saints, and even up to Jesus as he hung on a cross, crying out to his Father, "Why have you forsaken me?"

David, a man known for his worship for God, didn't hide his Cry, but instead used it to draw closer to God. Saying,

"But in my distress I cried out to the LORD; yes, I prayed to my God for help. He heard me from his sanctuary; my cry to him reached his ears."

We have a tendency to shy away from our passion, pain, and desperation, all the things that bring us to the edge of our humanity. Maybe we do this out of comfort, or maybe out of fear of the unknown. But I think we ought not, for in those moments and feelings, in those places of deep angst, I think we might just find what truly makes us human. What if we listened to this Cry within us? What if we acknowledged and embraced the times in our lives when we find ourselves pushed to the edge of our humanity? Maybe, just maybe, when we find ourselves at the end of our humanity, we will also find ourselves closer to the Divine.

I don't know how you might embrace the Cry inside of you – Lou does when he listens to opera. I do it when I listen to screamo and watch movies. And in the worst moments of my life, it wasn't the "everything is happy" lyrics that helped me, but instead the heavy music and desperate screams echoing the pain I felt inside that helped heal me.

In each of us we have a Cry, pushing us to the edge of our frail, mortal humanity, longing for something more. It lives and breathes in each Cry, reminding us that past the edge of our broken and temporal humanity lies something beautiful and eternal.

And one of the most amazing things is, God felt this very Cry – a cry so deep in His heart it pushed Him to the edge of His divinity and broke through to our fractured and temporal world, simply responding to the Cry within Him to be in connection to His creation.

So the next time you find yourself taking the emotional journey to the depths and edges of your soul, don't run. Don't cover your face. Lean into it and you just might discover God in it with you.

Chapter 8

Looking For Love Stories

"I don't think anybody ever forgets the first person
they fell in love with. That's something that
everybody remembers, and it doesn't matter what
the time period is or where; I mean, those feelings
are always the same."
- Rob Reiner

I was sitting in a fancy hotel room in Beverly Hills
with three other journalists. I was there because I had
taken an odd job as an online interviewer, and had
somehow wound up doing press interviews for the
highly-anticipated romantic movie coming out on
Valentine's Day. We sat around a table, awaiting our
turn to sit with and ask the stars of the movie
questions. In the minutes leading up to the interview,
the other writers sat there nervously, adjusting their

hair and fixing their clothes as they waited for the movie stars to walk in.

After what seemed like hours, the door opened, and in walked Channing and Rachel. No matter how many times you see someone famous in real life, it's always an interesting moment to experience someone in the flesh you have "known" for years on a screen. Channing was warm and friendly and Rachel was polite but quiet. They sat at the table with us and we began, one by one, taking turns asking them questions. Some of the questions my cohorts asked were light, like what it was like working together, and some were technical, like what the day-to-day on set was like. But knowing I only had a few minutes with the actors, since it was a movie about falling in and out of love, I asked a question that struck a bit deeper to the heart of humans and our affinity for love stories, a question that seems to pulse through the heart of every soul in the city, but really, the whole world. I cleared my throat, and with just a bit of nervous energy, I asked Channing why he thought love was valuable and something worth fighting for. He didn't immediately answer. I worried for a moment that I had dug too deep for an article about a romance flick people just wanted to escape into. But after a few seconds, he spoke. Interestingly enough, he began by expressing his regret and disappointment at the state of marriage and commitment today. He expressed his hopes that this movie would show real love. He said, "I don't think people go at it in the right way anymore, it's such a culture about right now, you know? Things that are supposed to bring us together, just make us further apart."

We all sat there in the pauses of his thoughts, thinking about the words he'd spoken. Finally, he finished with one last thought: "Even moral things, like how you want to raise children, I think that's the big hurdle when you get married. Everything's fine when you're together, then it comes time to raise a child."

A few moments later, the movie stars left. I sat there, pondering his words and deciding what I thought of what he had said. It was interesting to hear one of the most recognizable faces at the time, known by his stories in magazines, and movies on the silver screen, talk about how far we've wandered from what real love is — how we base it on such surface level things that can never bear the full weight of true love, while ignoring the actual values that keep love enduring.

That interview was almost a decade ago, and sadly, since then, both Channing and I experienced the death of what we thought was going to be a lifelong love. His, on a bigger stage, but mine, just as devastating on my modest platform.

I look back on those words he spoke, never thinking that they were to me. And perhaps, he never thought they would be words about himself. But the truth that laid inside of them still remains. Love is something valuable and rare, but it also seems fragile, and prone to destruction when it's not built on something deeper than what this shallow world says is sufficient.

~

I met a girl in my first month of living in Los Angeles. I was freshly into my twenties and she was eighteen. She was one of the worship singers at the young adult group at Bel-Air (yes, as in *The Prince of...*) Church, and I was the new kid. She started texting me, I started driving her to church, and we spent the next five years of our lives together – until a year after we got married, when everything fell apart.

I never thought I would be heartbroken and divorced at twenty five, much less at all. That wasn't how it was supposed to go. In the movies I had playing through my mind, the guy and the girl always end up together. They work it out, and love conquers everything. But this wasn't the movies, this was real life. And outside the trappings of polished cinematography, pithy dialogue, and a third act that fixes everything, I was left with the hauntingly disappointing reality of broken humans trying to catch and hold onto love, then fumbling it until it falls and breaks.

We as a people are obsessed with love. It's as if we are designed to desire it from the deepest places of our soul. We watch countless movies and TV shows about it, we download apps and spend hours swiping, trying to find it, we buy magazines to read about it in other people's lives. But despite being obsessed with finding it, it seems we aren't very good at keeping it. It's ironic that Hollywood, the very place that creates the love stories we all hold as images for how love is supposed to look, is the place known for broken relationships. For every sparkling summer romance flick, there's another ten relationships that fall apart in front of our eyes, splashed across trashy tabloids and paparazzi pictures. Why is this? How can we be a people so obsessed with something we are so bad at doing?

I think back over my time searching for love, trying to answer this deep call in my heart, and how often I've looked in the wrong places. In my mind, I had pictures from magazines and scenes from movies guiding what I ought to be looking for. But like Channing said, these things are just shallow imitations of real love, never getting to the heart of what actually makes a beautiful love an authentic and lasting thing.

~

I remember being excited when I got the news of who my first scene partner would be shortly after joining an acting class in the heart of Hollywood. I saw her for the first time sitting across the room in a pixie cut and a striped shirt, visibly ignoring me, the new kid. I walked over to her and laid my best one-liner on her. She tried not to smile, but I saw the corners of her mouth turn up.

The scene we would be rehearsing and performing was one that was reminiscent of one of the worst moments in my life: a devastating break up scene. And here I was, paired up with my crush. Over the next few weeks, I would look forward to receiving her texts, even if it was just about scheduling rehearsals. I would find reasons to reach out to her, asking her things I already knew about the scene, and upon figuring out her favorite Starbucks order, showed up to her house with it in hand, to which I got another, slightly bigger, half-smile – progress.

She was distant and seemed guarded, but I liked her. I knew that beneath the surface of the armor she wore, there was more to the mystery of her than met the eye.

One night, as I walked her home after class down Sunset Boulevard, by the endless headlights, we stopped for just a moment. I told her I had feelings for her. She shyly said she had feelings for me, too. I asked if I could kiss her. As the streetlight shone down on us, all alone in a crowded city, I kissed her, both of us bathed in a movie-like light.

Over the course of rehearsing and performing our scene together, gently, slowly but surely, connection was created. I began to find, behind her pretty face and cool demeanor, was a woman filled with emotion — hopes, dreams, and regrets. On the surface, she had seemed coy and cute, but upon being allowed into her world, I found more than I had bargained for.

In the season of courting this woman I had begun falling for, I found that she was more than my fantasy

made up of movie scenes and magazine covers. She
was more than a pretty face. This was both a
wonderful and terrifying thing. Anything of substance
is wonderful, but heavy. And with the history I was
shouldering into this new relationship, I was unsure if
I would be able to bear her weight, much less my own.
But in uncovering the inner world of this wide-eyed
woman, I found so many beautiful things that my soul
had been longing for. I discovered someone in her
who desired connection to God, loved great art,
reveled in the poetry of words, and yearned for a
future unbound by her past.

When I went through my divorce, I thought perhaps
I'd never love or be loved again. I suddenly
understood the appeal of the one-night stand —
getting what your body wants without risking harm to
your heart. I promised myself that I would look for
something easy and safe.

But here I was, in love with a woman who was neither.
She was a human — a complicated one, and that scared
me. But in seeing the deep rivers where our hearts,

values, and souls connected, I knew that this is what lasting and true love was made out of.

I came to a place where I had to decide: did I want the easy, skin-deep love the world advertises, free of complications and full of photoshopped fakeness? Or was I brave enough to dive into a love that had the markings of what I should've looked for all along, but would ask everything of me?

On November 11th, 2019, we eloped on a roof in New York City. I'll let you know if I made the right choice in heaven. But I know this: I didn't make the easy and safe one, like the world tells us we should. I made the one that is hard and scary, but I chose a woman who possessed with me the things that make love last.

~

Love isn't easy, but it was never supposed to be. It was instead designed to be beautiful, and anything truly beautiful takes time, effort, nuance, and dedication.

God handcrafted love to be a force of good in our dark world, but we so often buck His design and use it for destruction. But perhaps if we return to a valuable and substantive view of love, rejecting the easy, simple, and shallow love culture has offered us, we will find ourselves returning to what love was always made to be: a powerful, warm, and meaningful force that can breathe life back into a dying world, even a world like Hollywood.

Chapter 9

Yes, And...

"The world is a slightly better place for having improvisation in it than it was before. There's something about it that says something positive about the human spirit, that a bunch of people can get together and by following a few simple traffic rules can create art and can entertain an audience and can thrill and exalt each other."

- Del Close

There came a time in my journey through Hollywood when suddenly, it felt that my life and everything in it had stopped; that my existence slammed on the brakes and everything in my life came to a thudding halt. My emotions, relationships, dreams, and mind all seemed to fall apart at the same time, and to be honest, I didn't know what to do next.

I had recently gone through the most painful breakup I had ever experienced, watching the girl I loved for the past five years walk away. Followed by that, my ever-present mental illness hit an all-time high, creating a cloud of depression, obsession, and anxiety so thick I often wouldn't leave my apartment for days on end. On top of both my heart and mind failing, auditions were few and far between, and even when they did come, I just couldn't seem to book them.

It felt as if my life had just decided to give up on me and break down on the side of the road I had been traveling. And as much as I wanted to pretend everything was okay and I could just slap on a smile and keep going, I simply didn't feel I could.

So I did what any rational adult does when they need professional mental, emotional, relational, and vocational help: I signed up for an improv class.

I had always enjoyed watching improv, seeing a handful of performers outfitted in jeans and t-shirts on a blank stage bring scenes to life in front of our eyes, out of thin air, evoking childlike wonder and laughter. But in all my years in Hollywood, I never tried it out. Maybe it was because I was scared, or maybe it was because as an actor, I was more comfortable with knowing what comes next because it's written down in the script, or maybe I just thought I didn't need it. I was already a pretty funny guy, able to come up with one-liners pretty quickly, always being the class clown and family comedian. But for whatever reason, I suddenly felt it was time to try it out.

So on a warm summer afternoon in Hollywood, I found myself in a small room surrounded by twenty other young actors in Improv 101 at the Upright Citizens Brigade. Before we started, the teacher went over some basic rules for improv, a small and simple list of guidelines for us to follow and remember before we started creating our scenes. The guidelines included things like allowing ourselves to fail and to keep going anyway, to support our scene partners even when we were having a hard time, and the most important of all, "Yes, and..."

"Yes and..." is the number one rule of improv and is the core to any good scene or performer. It is essentially a twofold concept that in any scene with any partner we must learn to always say...

"YES": We don't deny our circumstances or try to manipulate them to make us feel more comfortable — meaning, if our scene partner says, "Oh no! The spaceship is broken!" We don't try to change the scene and say something like, "We're not in a spaceship, we're in the White House," but instead, we live in the "reality" around us and find the story within it. We don't deny, but accept fully. Once we learn to say, "yes," we then say...

"AND": We accept the circumstances we find ourselves in and we move forward, we add to the scene. We take the "truth" surrounding us and learn to create within the midst of it: "Yes, the spaceship is going down, *AND* it looks like I'm the only one who can fix it! Where's my laser toolkit?!"

All good improv scenes are predicated upon this, "Yes, and..." rule.

The teacher, knowing we were all new to improv, was kind and patient as we awkwardly but earnestly tried our hand at creating scenes out of thin air together. But even as we, inexperienced, self-conscious, baby performers, fumbled our way through practice scenes in a small classroom, week by week, we learned to, "Yes, and..." each other, and our scenes were a little better every time. Eventually, we had come to the end of the twelve weeks arrived at our class show, held in the legendary Upright Citizens Brigade Theatre in Hollywood, where some of the most famous comedians and actors in the world had performed, where for the first time, we got to be real improv performers and take a shot at creating our own scenes from thin air together for all the world to see.

There was a nervous energy as we sat in the legendary green room backstage. We cracked jokes and smiled at each other, waiting for the music to come on and the announcer to call us onstage. But with it, there was also an innocent excitement, knowing that the show we were about to put on would be the first and last of its kind, a magic that would take place only once in the history of the world — and this magic would happen in our hands, armed with the confidence of the, "Yes, and..." to guide us.

When we finally did shuffle out onto the small stage, looking out into the dark black box theater where a group of people in search of a half hour of laughs had gathered, we were all smiles and nerves. We asked the audience for a suggestion to get us started. From the dark of the room, we heard, "handkerchief!" and, leaving all our fear behind, we jumped right into the beauty of adults playing make believe. For the next half hour, we created, shaped, and lived in a story of our own design.

There, on a small stage armed with only our imaginations and willingness to create something magical, we played. Our scenes weren't perfect — they had awkward silences that went on too long, crossed wires, and jokes that didn't quite land, but through it, we kept moving. We kept on *Yes, and*-ing each other until a scene was made.

~

After the class, performances, and congratulatory smiles were through and I went back to my real life, I found that the, "Yes, and..." mantra lingered with me, staying in my mind and working its way into my daily life. I was still in the same place I had been in, still in the same scene I had just a couple months earlier, still dealing with the reality of a slowing career, an uncontrollable mind, and a broken heart — but somehow, after spending three months learning to say, "Yes, and..." I felt like I was going to be okay, like I was going to make it.

In the morning, when I would wake up, I would stare at my ceiling and as I prayed to God I would say, "YES, I am struggling and I keep on making mistakes, and I'm having a really hard time... but I'm going to say, AND today, I'm going to add something to my scene."

I think God loves it when we say, "Yes, and..." — He's not so much worried about the mistakes we make, or the lines we fumble along the way, just that we will learn to accept the circumstances we find ourselves inside and our ability to say yes to the scene we're in.

It's not always easy, and very often it's filled with missteps and awkward moments, but with God's help, we don't have to be stuck in a dead end scene. We can choose to say, "Yes, and..." and with Him, in spite of the reality we are in, create a beautiful story that the world has never seen before and will never see again.

We need only learn to say, "Yes, and..."

Chapter 10

Almost Famous

"Show me an actor who doesn't want to be famous,
and I'll show you a liar. Later, you realize that
there's more to it than just the acquisition of fame,
and money and girls. But that is what drives them
and was what drove me, initially."
- Kevin Bacon

On a warm day on the outskirts of Los Angeles, I
excitedly walked towards the set, having booked my
first role in a *movie* — a real movie, with real cameras,
lights, and movie stars. I only had a small part, but I
was *a part* of it, nonetheless.

I walked past the row of trailers and the bustling crew,
directly into the place where the magic would be
happening. After getting signed in, and going through
wardrobe and makeup, I decided to take a secret tour

through the movie set I would be acting on in a few short hours. Sneaking away, I inched my way carefully to and through the space, taking in the world the set designers and prop masters had created for the movie set. I stood, looking at all the movie magic around me, excited for my turn to be a part of it. A couple of voices shook me out of my trance, and I noticed a few people standing off to the side. I approached a short woman wearing a black hoodie, who I assumed to be an assistant. I said hello and started making small talk. I told her I was excited to be on set and she kindly smiled and small talked back. Suddenly, an unseen voice yelled out.

"That's lunch!"

The out-of-sight Production Assistant was letting everyone know it was time to eat before we started filming. I was a bit lost and a little disoriented as people started passing through on their way to catering. So I asked the woman in the hoodie if she would walk me to where I was supposed to be. She kindly agreed, and we began the long walk to the dining tent. We exchanged names and talked about this and that – where her accent was from, where I lived, and how she got involved with the production. When we reached the tables, I thanked her and went to find some food before sitting down with my new friends I had made from hair and makeup. Upon sitting down, the makeup artist looked at me, wide-eyed, and asked if I knew who I'd just been talking to. I said I didn't, and that I thought she must've been just a Production Assistant. He guffawed, then with a smirk, let me know I had been walking with the star of the movie, one of Hollywood's leading ladies. Garbed in the hoodie, not made up or on the silver screen, I hadn't recognized her. But I was suddenly struck by how gracious she had been to this no-name, young actor who didn't even recognize her, much less give her the treatment she was entitled to.

~

I wish I could say that when I moved to Hollywood, I did it with perfect motives. But for better or worse, I'm human. I, of course, did have the desire to make movies that changed the world for the better, to use my talents selflessly for God and His purposes. But long before I even began my trek to Los Angeles, there was something else creeping into the back of my mind. There was another small but powerful voice whispering things in my ear. Yes, I had good intentions, but I also wanted to be a "star." I know that doesn't seem too bad on the surface — I mean, it's a part of our everyday cultural vocabulary. We hear news and gossip about the "stars," we laud them with attention, money, and adoration. What could be so bad, right?

I figured it couldn't hurt to want to be famous and popular. Which of us doesn't? But as I lived, worked, and looked at the city and the people in it, I began to see the darker side of seeking stardom, one that fosters selfishness, envy, and defining ourselves by superficial things. Chasing stardom easily becomes an addiction that leads to destruction and ultimately separates us from God. But the scariest thing of all is that even after seeing all that, I still wanted it.

No, I *still want* it. I want to be liked. I want to be famous. I want people to think I'm the most interesting and talented person in the room. When in groups of people, I catch myself trying to convince them how great I am by dropping bits of my resume in search of reactions. Even now, writing this book, I do it with good motives — but there's still a part of me that wants you to think I'm cool, important, and smart.

Humility isn't something that's often talked about or displayed in Hollywood — at least not compared to the regular displays of money, status, and power. But it's one that is regularly talked about from Jesus, who like the movie star in the hoodie, didn't demand the esteem he was entitled to, but while being God of all Creation, humbled himself to walk with the low-class sinners, and nobody actors like me.

~

I can remember going to a church right in the heart of Los Angeles. It was surrounded by sidewalks covered with the names of once-famous and forgotten people etched into bronze stars you had to step over to get inside.

The interior of the church was cool, sleek, and attractive, and so were its people. I remember my first roommate telling me that in Los Angeles, you needed to submit a headshot before you went to the popular churches so they could make sure you were pretty enough to sit in their pews. Funny, but sadly, not too far off.

You could hear the music thumping through the lobby before you even stepped foot into the chapel. The worship band was loud and impressive, coupled with a concert-grade light show and sometimes, even smoke. Pretty girls in skinny jeans raised their hands on stage, as slick videos with popular worship song lyrics played behind them.

I immediately wanted to be a part of this group. So for the next few months, I tried to get to know people, show off my best side, wear my coolest clothes, hoping to fit in, hoping to get to rub shoulders with one of the celebrities that frequented the services. All the while, I was ignoring feeling inside of me that told me something was askew. I realize now that when I went to this church, it didn't feel all that different than when I went to auditions or "Hollywood parties" – there was a strong sense of insecurity, competition, cliques, and clear lines of who the popular kids were and weren't. But I didn't pay attention to that feeling, only the thoughts of making it to the in crowd... of church.

But after months of attempting to be one of the cool kids, something finally pulled the rose-colored glasses off and I saw more clearly why I had to leave. For weeks, both in and out of service, the pastor had been advertising an event he was putting on with the church. It had something to do with charity, but it was mostly sold with the names of the celebs hosting. It cost $40 to go, and not wanting to miss out on the fun, I quickly bought my ticket.

When the night arrived, I very insecurely pulled my old Ford Focus to the front of the fancy Hollywood hotel where the event was taking place. I had put on my coolest sport coat (from Goodwill), carefully molded my hair, and spritzed with my best cologne in an effort to fit in with the crowd. Me and my date snuck a picture on the red carpet after the invited celebs, one of whom was Kim Kardashian, had been ushered away. We then excitedly walked in.

Inside was a sight to behold, as hundreds of beautiful people mingled, cocktails in hand, servers passed out gourmet hors d'oeuvres, and famous people walked the large halls in their expensive suits and low-cut dresses. We got a picture with a popular E! News host and basked in the decadent affair, enjoying the feeling of importance that had only cost $40 – until the entertainment portion started.

We were escorted into a large room by security personnel dressed in tuxedos. As I ushered me and my date closer to the front, suddenly we were stopped, unable to move any closer to the stage. In front of us was a divider blocking our way forward. Beyond the divider was a section roped off for the "VIPs." It was filled with couches, bottles of champagne, and the best view of the stage. I saw a couple members of a popular boy-band just a few feet in front of me lounging on the leather sofas, enjoying themselves, as a celebrity host walked on stage with our "pastor" to get the night started. I had all but forgotten the event was for a charity cause to help the poor. I couldn't help but wonder who this event was *actually* for. So my date and I stood for the rest of the night with the other second-class crowd as we watched the VIPs hobnob with the ones either important or rich enough to be on the right side of the rope. Eventually, my date got tired of standing in heels and I got tired of watching people pat themselves on the back at an event where the people who were "being helped" most likely wouldn't have been let in.

I drove home that night feeling more clearly the insecurity, frustration, and reality of what popularity and fame can do. It was just a little later after finding out that our pastor had a personal makeup artist and a security team tasked to keep people from talking to him in church that I decided to take my leave. But it struck me how long it had taken me to realize this place had very little to do with the gospel they were claiming.

As I think about Jesus, a dusty, homeless, poor, rough-handed, dark-skinned, Middle Eastern man living in the desert, hanging out with crazy people and prostitutes, I have to wonder if he would have been let in that night... probably not.

I have spent many years in Los Angeles, a place where, daily, as I walk down the street, I am confronted with a barrage of flashing billboards covered with beautiful faces and promises of becoming the next "big thing," a place where I have spent the last five years working towards becoming an actor, finding myself in countless conversations at auditions, on sets, at restaurants, even churches, about finding that "big break" that will finally bring the attention we came here to find.

I have spent time with famous people, while watching adoring fans fawn uncontrollably, hoping for pictures and autographs. I have watched as paparazzi risk their lives running in front of traffic just to get a snap of a passing movie star.

Even beyond Hollywood, as I open my laptop or turn on my phone, I am faced with the realization that we are a generation obsessed with fame and popularity. We count our worth by the numbers on a screen, spending hours and days crafting the image ourselves we present to the digital world in the hopes of attracting more people to "follow," "like," and "share" us. Every click serves as a fix, as a high. We so desperately long to validate the identity we are building for ourselves as "influencers."

And If I'm being completely honest, I want it – all of it. I want people to think I'm a big deal, someone worth jumping in front of traffic for a glimpse of, or worthy of a billboard. I want the satisfaction of knowing that my life is important enough to obsess over, and the knowledge that I am someone important.

And the thing is, in a world that can so often tear us apart, leave us feeling beaten up, insecure, unimportant, and unseen, of course it would be our natural inclination to find approval in a place that offers us a chance at validation, as temporary and hollow as it is. We look at our screens and magazines and see everything we don't have, but long to be: put together, taken care of, adored, validated, respected, and loved.

But recently, as I studied the arguably most famous person in all of human history, Jesus, I found something very surprising. I found a man who called himself "humble and meek," a man who claimed to be God incarnate, performing inexplicable miracles, but would do so hesitantly because of a crowd, saying, "It's not my time," a man who, after bringing someone back to life, told them to, "tell no one," and a man who, when in the middle of a roaring crowd, would disappear to be alone. Jesus treated everyone, regardless of title, sex, or age, with the same respect and dignity. He chose to spend most of his time not on a stage, but eating, talking, and living with the poor, needy, dirty, broken, and outcast.

I was shocked. The most influential person in history was the most humble.

After coming to this realization, I saw how different the priorities of ours are to that of Jesus'. Even the ones who call themselves followers of his – daily, I watch as Christian bloggers relentlessly vie and scheme for more hits and followers, as Christian figures tout pictures of themselves with pop stars. I spectate as Christian companies use Jesus as a marketing tool to sell more shirts, movies, and music, while popular pastors soak up attention like rock stars, as they stand in bright lights in front of big screens and thumping music. And all of it makes me wonder, if Jesus were here today, where would he actually be found?

I have come to the conclusion that I don't think God cares about celebrities. He cares about people. Don't get me wrong – I think fame can be used for good, and popularity for a positive effect, but more often than not, we create it into an idol to be worshiped instead of a tool to be used. And in the end, the only thing God cares about is our hearts.

What would it look like if, instead of working to build more popularity or an "online presence," we worked towards kindness? How would we change if we put a little less effort into racking up accomplishments, and instead made moral decisions when no one is watching and "likes" aren't a possibility? What would it look like if, instead of trying so hard to be considered a VIP, we made those around us the very important people? Could it be that perhaps we would begin to find true validation in who we were created to be, and not the facade we are trying to create?

There's a certain freedom to be found in the truth that the creator of the universe doesn't care about your status, bank account, accomplishments, or popularity, but instead, simply cares about you. That His main concern isn't your outward appearance, but instead, the condition of your heart.

And while, another "like," and a new line on a resume is nice, how beautiful is it to know that regardless of anything you can do, the creator of the universe adores you, to the point of giving His life for you? A realization of this magnitude will forever outweigh any fading accolade from this world.

Chapter 11

Church Cinema

"The point I'm trying to make is that you go to church on Sunday. But the real Christ is out there in your life every day, whether it be the guy you help on the street, how you live your life, and your countenance that makes people want to be you."

- Jim Caviezel

The neon lights above us blinked and bounced off our skin. Each and every one of us excitedly walked off the cold streets and packed into a warm, gigantic theater for a midnight movie showing. The theater was enormous and still somehow barely fit the hundreds in attendance to sit in front of a screen that seemed to stretch for miles. Everyone in that theater came from different places, backgrounds, and ways of life. There were old and young, there were poor and rich, there were atheists and believers, there were progressives and conservatives, there black and white, and there were women and men – groups seemingly so different, but ultimately, each there for the same reason: we loved and felt a part of this story.

My philosopher (and podcast co-host) friend, Joseph, who moonlights as a film critic, loves both movies and people. So in an effort to combine his favorite things, he invited a big group of actors, artists, writers, thinkers, and fellow story-lovers to go to the premiere of the final Avengers movie. I had been watching these superhero movies for over a decade, and if you know me at all, you know that since I've been a young boy, I have had a special place in my heart for superheroes. Their stories carried me through some of the hardest times of my life, and inspired me in the good ones to fight for the best version of myself. So naturally, I jumped at the chance to experience the end of an era surrounded by my friends at a midnight showing of *Avengers: Endgame*.

There was an excited energy as the clock struck twelve. Smells of fresh popcorn filled the air as sounds of shuffling bodies and excited whispers rumbled just beneath the music that suddenly came blaring through the room. Like a big bang, the movie began, and for the next few hours, the hundreds of souls filling that theater in New York City were united as we entered this grand story together.

Being so lost in the moment, I almost didn't catch the magical thing that was happening that night. I almost didn't see the beauty of this diverse congregation beautifully connecting over one epic story. As the third act of the movie flashed across the screen, when all the heroes crested the hill, united and readying themselves to overthrow the dark armies of evil in the universe, with music swelling and heroes posed, suddenly the entire theater burst into a roaring cheer – people were out of their seats, clapping their hands, and celebrating this moment, because the good guys won. It was then, as I turned my head to see both my friends and strangers living in this magical moment together, that I suddenly realized, this wasn't just a movie – this was church.

~

Don't worry, I know it wasn't actually church. But as I look back on that night and the nights before it, stretching back all the way to when I was a kid dressing up as a Middle Earth warrior to see the midnight showing of *The Lord of the Rings: The Return of the King*, I see how powerfully good and true stories unify and connect us. I see the strand that weaves its way through all of humanity, causing us to find – beyond all the trappings and definitions of this world – the fulfillment to a longing place deep inside all of us. A longing to be a part of something bigger than us all, a meaningful story. And it's in this realization I find myself wishing church could be the same. Because in my heart of hearts, beyond all the logic, arguments, and proof, the reason I am a man of faith, the reason I follow God and have given my whole life to Christ, is because I was given an epic story to be a part of. Like the myths I grew up reading on pages of books and watching across theater screens, I was given the one true Myth that invites me to take part in its epic story, one that has been unfolding since the dawn of time. I am a Christian because I was made to love and desire good stories. And God's creation and redemption of the world is a good story, one I want to be a part of.

And as I think about why I gave my life to God and why I am still inspired, daily, to live in this beautiful story God is telling, I can't help but see that contrasted by what the church has so often become.

In the few decades I have been alive, I have seen churches take on the toxicity of the world it lives in, so often becoming more known for what it stands against than what it stands for. Many churches today have become exclusionary, moralistic, tribalistic, or even worse, boring. We have reactively erased the beauty that comes from taking part in a grand story together and have turned our focus, from the grand narrative that is Christianity, to lifeless moral lists, culture wars, and fear-mongering. In doing this, we have become bland and — dare I say it — lukewarm. We have forgotten the childlike wonder of becoming obsessed with an awesome story alongside our closest friends.

Humans are intrinsically story-driven people, which ultimately means that humans, like it or not, are intrinsically religious people. Which is why I can't help but wonder if the recent statistics of young people leaving the church is tied to the very fact that we have lost the skill for seeing and sharing the grand story that lives in God's words. Young people, like myself, long to be a part of something bigger than ourselves, a story that gives our lives meaning, and our decisions purpose. But in finding that the church has lost the art of telling that story well, I see my generation trading what is the greatest story, told badly, for lesser stories, told better.

~

A few Sundays ago, I found myself in a church I had never been to before. The pews felt hard and uncomfortable as I sat down, taking in the smell of slightly-rotting wood wafting through the old AC unit. The clean people around me kept mostly to themselves, aside from their quick glances in my direction, making me suddenly realize that my jeans left me underdressed in the sea of pressed slacks and long dresses. Eventually the music began, being led by a middle-aged woman in a floral skirt and a tired looking pianist while the congregants, holding worn hymnals, sang along in monotone and muted emotion. When the last off-key "Hallelujah" was sung, we sat down and listened to a bald man wander through classic verses, tying them into something vaguely political, finishing with another rendition of the first hymn. I walked out of there tired. Worn, even. I so badly wanted this place, the place that represents the grand story I have given my life to, to show even a glimpse of the awesomeness of God's tale. But it simply didn't. I found myself thinking back to the night I watched the last Avengers movie with my friends. I thought of all the excitement and unifying energy, I thought of the utter diversity and unity found in the room that night, and how little of those things I had found in the whitewashed walls of the church that day.

~

The church is a beautiful and meaningful place based on a beautiful and meaningful story. And for some reason, God left it in the hands of fallible human beings who are so often prone to tribalism, pettiness, and mistakes. But that doesn't take away the power it could have. For many today, the church has become stale, lifeless, and sometimes even hostile. So they've gone in search of a better, more welcoming and captivating story, be that in Hollywood, movie theaters, TV shows, or political groups, all of whom have capitalized on the basic human need for story by casting their own narratives for people to take part and act in. But I do have hope — there was a time when the church was making and creating the greatest and most inspiring art in the world, a time when the church was leading the front on beauty and reflecting the grand story in ways that so strongly drew in those who were exposed to it. One look at Michelangelo's Sistine Chapel stretching out over all who gaze up to see its dazzling wonders, filled with colors and characters, and it's almost impossible to not want to be a part of the story that inspired this work.

~

Years ago, my friend and fellow movie, videogame, and story lover friend, Brandon, invited me to something called Wondercon. Just outside the city limits of Los Angeles, Wondercon was a convention where all the best movies, TV shows, video games, and books were celebrated by thousands of people for three days. Upon arriving, I was immediately wrapped up in the world. I was surrounded by incredible cosplayers gilded in intricate and ornate costumes modeled after their favorite characters from their favorite stories. I passed Luke Skywalkers, Optimus Primes, Wonderwomen, and so on and so forth. The convention hall was filled to the brim with creative energy, bursting from every booth displaying beautiful art, innovative video games, and new comic books and novels to get lost inside of. But just before I entered all the "wonder" that lay inside, I had passed a small group of people outside on the steps. They weren't dressed in magical costumes or wearing excited smiles. Instead they were gilded in uniform, mustard polos and grimaces. Each held a sign with angry capital letters scrawled across it: "SIN BRINGS GOD'S WRATH." I shuddered seeing this sight. I stopped for just a second, taking in the glaring juxtaposition of people speaking for and representing the imaginative God of the universe with boring, sardonic, angry signs, in a place filled with people celebrating stories in colorful, inviting, and beautiful ways.

If I didn't know the beauty of God and I was confronted with an option between which story, which religion, I wanted to take part in, it wouldn't even be a choice.

~

People are inherently religious. We see it in theaters as we gather together to worship and take part in the mass of an epic movie; we see it at Wondercon, where we adorn ourselves in grand vestiments to celebrate our favorite tales through rituals of remembrance and reflection; we see it world over through the faithful people who attend church, some in huts, some in cathedrals, to further enter this story God has given us. And being people who are intrinsically religious, we are intrinsically story-oriented. We long for a great and grand epic to be a part of, one that invites us all –

every tribe, tongue, and nation – to take part in all the
glorious narrative God has created the universe inside
of. I have this vision of church being every bit as
inviting, captivating, and beautiful as anything this
world could produce – I have a vision that the awe
and excitement of a film premiere in a movie theater
can happen every Sunday in an old church.

God's story is the most beautiful, most inspiring, most
adventurous, most redemptive, most creative story to
ever be told, but until the world encounters that
beauty, it will continue to look for or try to create a
better one.

Chapter 12

To Be Known

"Fame is not external, it's internal. So I've been famous for a long time."
- Lady Gaga

I remember arriving late to church one evening and seeing a memorable sight. As I stepped into the foyer trying to catch my breath, the door to the sanctuary opened, and along with the muffled thumping of worship music, a young woman walked through the door. It took me a moment before I registered who it was that had just entered the empty lobby with me: a movie star — one of the biggest in the world at that time. I didn't immediately recognize her because the context I was used to seeing her in was absent. There

were no flashing lights or red carpets around. She
wasn't holding an award, but instead her child,
pushing their head firmly against her chest. She wasn't
dressed in a beautiful, low-cut gown, but instead a
T-shirt and jeans. She wasn't on the cover of an
airbrushed magazine or perfectly-lit screen, but
instead she was standing right in front of me.
Suddenly she ceased to be a romanticized fantasy that
lived only in my (and the rest of the world's) mind.
She was a real, flesh and blood, human being. She
looked at me. In her eyes was trepidation; she seemed
worried I might disturb her escape into the quiet,
perhaps with a request for an autograph or selfie. But I
just smiled. She smiled back and walked outside.

~

I have one famous friend — Tom. We met in acting
school, bonding over a shared sense of absurd humor
and being teenagers with big dreams of becoming
stars. Tom is from France and comes from a beloved
family of famous actors and singers. An entire
generation of Parisians grew up watching his family in
their films and on their stages. Not being French, I

didn't immediately believe Tom when he told me this — until I witnessed him get stopped in the street multiple times by European tourists asking for pictures. Now, more than a decade later, I watch from afar as Tom appears in French TV shows and movies, his face gracing the cover of popular European Magazines, and as hundreds of thousands of fans follow, comment, and vie for his attention. It's an interesting phenomenon, watching someone you know as a real person, who pulled all-nighters exploring the city, told stupid jokes in apartments, and swapped stories about crushes, become a fantasy in the eyes of a crowd. Recently, on a rooftop bar while Tom was visiting the US, I teased him about his adoring public, knowing the real, goofy, kindhearted man beneath the gloss of public image. He humbly dismissed the attention and told me that he tells a story about me on every talk show he goes on. I smiled.

~

I grew up with my own modicum of fame as well. While my family were hardly movie stars or pop sensations, my mother was a best-selling author whose books revolved around stories about me and the rest of my family. We grew up putting on conferences around the country, and sometimes the world, for thousands of people who had read all of our stories and came for a chance to see us in person. I remember being surprised as a kid, then getting used to, having multitudes of mostly 30-something moms coming up to me asking me to sign books and get pictures, asking very personal questions, wanting to know more about me and my family, and sometimes breaking down and crying as they shared their life stories that connected to mine in some way, shape, or form. This was a lot for a kid to handle. On one hand, I loved it — I loved being the center of attention, having people give me their adoration, wanting to know *me*. But on the other hand, it became scary that the image these people had of me in their mind, the one of a perfect Christian boy who came from the idyllic family, who offered them hope for their own, would crack, and they would see that I was just as sinful, human, and silly as anyone else. Even now, as an adult, after having written my own books and acted in my own movies, I receive countless messages from strangers who have come to know me through my life online, on a screen, or on a page, pouring out their hearts to me, wanting to know and hear from me. And while I'm filled with honor and joy that I am someone people *want* to know and connect to, I'm also fearful that if they knew the real me – the doubting, sinful, inconsistent, human Nathan – the letters would stop. I want the attention. I want to be known... but only part of me.

~

We live in a culture obsessed with fame, which I've touched on already, but it's more than that. It's more than just the desire for attention we've already explored. Many major outlets, blogs, and comment sections seem to shrug this obsession with "becoming famous" as people just wanting to be liked or be rich or paid attention to. And perhaps there's some truth to those aspects of it. But the desire for fame goes deeper than the surface-level want for attention. The desire for fame is ultimately a desire to be known and validated on a large scale for who we are – or at least the parts of ourselves we like. We were created by a

God who made us to both know Him and be known *by* Him. This is the most basic human need after survival. This is why infants instinctively immediately reach out to find their mother when they are born. That reach is something we never stop doing. We have a deep longing, whether we're aware of it or not, to be known and loved for who we are known as. This is why fame is so alluring. When we see thousands of adoring fans obsessing over a celebrity, we see someone who people are desiring to know and be known by. And more than anything, we wish to be known. We think that somehow, if we had thousands of adoring fans obsessing over every part of our lives, that we could satiate that deep soul-longing we've all felt from the day we took our first breath.

But the reality is, the people we think we know through movies, magazines, or TV shows aren't actually the people we think they are. That's an image, a fantasy, of a person that doesn't actually exist. The real people aren't photoshopped, airbrushed, and scripted. They're human beings with flaws, fears, and failures, mixed in with the beautiful. We desire fame because it represents being known for all of the shiny and wonderful things about us, but those things aren't the totality of any of us.

~

In the last decade, a movement referred to as, "cancel culture" has arisen, whereby formerly beloved public figures are taken down in public ways. Actors, singers, politicians, and celebrities we know and love are suddenly and swiftly being canceled when the news of their human failings are made known. The rose colored glasses have come off and we've suddenly started seeing that there are no perfect figures, regardless of what the late-night interviews and glossy pictures tell us. The image of these completely fantastical figures has been shattered. We have started to have a new understanding of fame – one that doesn't just make us suspect of the people we watch on screen, but ourselves as well. Fame loses its allure when we realize that it brings with it not just the nice parts of ourselves being known, but the ugly, broken, and dark parts we hope no one will ever see, lest we be cast out. The draw of fame is to be known; the fear of fame is to be fully known.

There's a temptation to gleefully join the mob as we point and scoff at a celebrity's fall from grace. This is often rooted in our hidden envy — they had the attention and gaze we so deeply desire. But if we are honest with ourselves, while we long to be seen and known, we live with the fear that if we actually were, we, like them, would be canceled, too. While we so want to be known, we are all too aware of our own personal mistakes, failures, and messy and broken bits. We then live with a need to be known, and the fear that we might *truly* be — and then, as a result, be rejected.

~

There's a story about Jesus meeting a woman at a well. She knew all too well the desire to be known, having found herself with a list of multiple husbands and lovers. Many religious people would reduce her promiscuity to simple "sinful desires" but as we see, more than just cheap thrills, she was searching for the fulfillment of one of her (and our) deepest needs: to be known. But the regretful decisions she had made on her search left her with skeletons in her closet, a scarlet letter she needed to hide. But Jesus, being God, told her he knew everything about her; he detailed her mistakes, misdeeds, and missteps, bringing them to the painful light of day. But he didn't stop there. He didn't see her mistakes and leave because of them. He offered her a new way forward — a way for both her fears of being unlovable and being unknown to be answered by him. Jesus offered her a chance at being fully known and fully loved.

~

When we come in contact with God, our Creator, we suddenly find, like Adam and Eve in the Garden, that we are naked and unable to hide from him. Our broken and messy parts are exposed, leaving us vulnerable. This keeps many people away from God, unwilling to risk the opportunity of getting hurt when their humanity is laid bare. But in scripture, we find that when we are brave enough to stand before Him, scars and all, we ultimately find only love. Like the woman at the well, God, the only One who can, offers us a way to be fully known and fully loved.

There's a 90's DC Talk song called, "What If I Stumble?" which details the conflicting desires of wanting fame, adoration, and to be known, but also the fear of what would happen if the crowd saw the singer for who they truly were — saw them when they fell. This dichotomous reality lives in all of us. It's something we wrestle with our entire lives, and the desire for fame is ultimately rooted in this intrinsic human need. But God tells us we need not strive after the affection of either fame nor lovers to be known, as He has created us and knows even the deepest most hidden parts of who we are. He also tells us, while seeing and knowing everything about us, that we are fully and truly loved. Grasping this truth about ourselves and the reality of our Creator will free us up to live as fully known, fully loved people.

Chapter 13

Creators Too

"We have our factory, which is called a stage. We make a product, we color it, we title it, and we ship it out in cans."

- Cary Grant

I stared at the blank screen, hoping my intense glare would coerce it into filling itself with inspired words. It stared back, unmoved. I was sitting in my room inside an old apartment I shared with four other guys, in the middle of North Hollywood. It was hot outside, as the San Fernando Valley heat had come in, sitting on the area like a blanket. As I frustratedly wiped another bead of sweat from my cheek, I muttered a swear word, it being the only word that actually seemed effective at the moment.

For the months and years leading up to this moment, I had been living the life as a starving artist-actor — a line here, an extra role there. But after my last one-word line in a TV show, I finally paid attention to the tugging in my heart for more. I had moved here wanting to be a part of great stories and films being made, but one line or small part here or there was no longer doing it for me. I wanted more. And even when I *did* have more than a line, the shows and movies I was cast in seemed so silly, trite, and meaningless in juxtaposition to the films I had watched and dreamed of being a part of as a kid — the kind of films that touched hearts and moved minds, the kind of stories that mattered and inspired their viewers to believe in more.

So I decided to write my own screenplay, make my own movie. If Hollywood had decided to not cast me in roles or projects that inspired my mind and heart, I would just have to make my own. But it turned out that envisioning myself writing a story from scratch was so much easier than actually doing it. I knew I wanted to tell a story. I just didn't know which one. But nonetheless, I was going to start this journey of creating something great, come hell or highwater.

~

I remember making my own movies as a kid with my friends. There were lots of bad costumes, plastic swords, and stolen story lines, but there was also heart, excitement, and a childlike innocence in bringing something good to life.

My favorite film of ours was one we made when I was thirteen. My friend Andrew directed and I starred (of course). Through weeks of free afternoons, about a thousand takes on a small digital camera that shot only fifteen seconds of video at time, and a month of editing, we made a short film. It was a very artsy, highbrow piece about me playing myself in a game of chess — a concept we didn't fully grasp, but knew meant something deep. It was a silent film, black and white, and set to Chopin's "Revolutionary Etude." It was simple and imperfect, but it was ours. And I was a part of bringing something into existence that hadn't been there before.

When the film was complete, to celebrate, we had a movie "premiere," the very first one I'd ever attended. We invited our families, poured cups of juice, dressed up, and crowded into the upstairs of an old house, around a small screen in my friend's bedroom. With the lights shut off, we watched our finished work with pride and joy. It didn't play to millions of screaming fans or break any box office records — instead it was played to a small but enthusiastic group of beaming kids and grinning adults. But the little film we played that night, the film we had put our whole hearts and minds into creating, was a step into me becoming who I was created to be: a co-creator.

~

Eventually, the words came. And there, in my rundown apartment building, I started crafting my very first script. I wasn't seasoned or experienced. I had no formal training or accredited education, just a desire to create something ex nihilo, out of my mind, that I could revel in and take joy from. Like a child with a marker attempting to paint a masterpiece, I gave it my all, and two weeks later, I had my first draft.

It was filled with plot holes, stunted dialogue, and spelling errors. But that didn't matter at that moment. As I typed the words, "the end," I finally sat back, basking in my accomplishment, and said to myself, "It is good." It wasn't perfect, but I had finally taken the first step towards acting in the image of my Creator, the grand storyteller Himself, and created something — an imperfect and flawed but passion-filled story, which I didn't know at the time would change my life.

A year later, I found myself on the set of the movie I had written, ready to bring it to life. And a year after that, I released my film for the world to see.

~

Searching through scripture, flipping all the way back to the beginning, I'm struck that the first time we meet God is as a Creator. In the first few chapters of Genesis, we see God as an artist, an architect, an engineer. The first movements we ever see God take are ones of creation, bringing life into voids, bringing order into chaos, bringing beauty and light into darkness. We watch with bated breath as God Himself casts stars into the sky, oceans across the land, and then creates man, who He says is made in His very own image.

We each see God in so many different ways; some see Him as a mean authoritarian boss, others as an absent father, and others as an indifferent, still, and unmoving computer. And how we see God is inextricably tied to how we see ourselves. But how would seeing God as He shows Himself in Genesis – as a creator, an artist who put thought and passion into His creations – change not only how we see Him, but ourselves?

It would mean we're not just a random happenstance, or an annoying and disappointing kid. It would mean we are works of art, worthy of value; beautiful, and covered in meaning. But how much *more* would it change how we saw ourselves and our callings if we took to heart the truth God spoke – that we are actually made in His image? Not just creations, but instead self-portraits, upon which each of us bear God's, the Creator's, image.

Chapter 14

All the Smoke & Lights

"The more I study religions, the more I am convinced that man never worshiped anything but himself."
- Richard Burton

I stepped into a lobby filled with pretty people, brushing past me with an air of stylish indifference. They seemed to move in fast motion, gilded in name brand shirts, slim fit jeans, and stylish hats. Around the packed lobby, banners hung, covered with catchy and inviting but trite quotes, equaling a message of, "Welcome." After a moment of taking in the room, I suddenly became aware of my secondhand clothes from GoodWill. Feeling a bit out of place, I headed into the "sanctuary." Walking through the door, I was quickly confronted with flashing lights, thick smog, and thumping bass, like a scene out of a club, but with slightly less cleavage. I made my way down the aisles of chairs to one in the far corner where I could observe, undisturbed. Taking my seat, I gazed up at the stage, boasting an IMAX-size screen projecting postmodern shapes, bouncing to the thumping of the music. Eventually the "service" began, after a set of attractive musicians strutted to their places like models down a runway, slammed the first note on their instruments at a volume that would rival a Fall Out Boy concert. Like a scene out of House of Blues, fog filled the room, obscuring the shapes of fit people raising their hands and mouthing the words to a worship song that sounded eerily like the recent Coldplay single. After an entertaining forty-five minutes of music, a speaker came out (or a preacher, or a spiritual influencer – I'm not sure what the slang is these days). After a sharply-cut video about their new app that you could now donate money on, he began his sermon/recitation of inspirational Instagram quotes.

He wore a trendy outfit, complete with a leather jacket and sneakers that I later found out cost close to one thousand dollars. The sermon wasn't bad — there were lots of encouraging bits, I was told how wonderful I was and encouraged to "keep going." I slipped out the back as the last song played, hoping to avoid the crowd of three thousand people leaving, feeling just a little guilty I didn't download the church app.

I had gone there that day looking for something. It had been a chaotic year in Los Angeles, in the smog of pursuing my dream and failing over and over at achieving it, mixed with a broken heart and the appearance of newly-formed bad habits that were teetering on the edge of addiction, I had found myself feeling lost, lonely, and far away from God. I had been told this church was the best; it had the coolest services, best music, and highest rate of celeb sightings. I didn't hate it — I had been entertained for an hour and enjoyed the music, but as I left, I realized nothing in my heart had changed. I didn't find the wisdom I longed for. I didn't feel closer to God. I felt the same. I had been distracted for an hour from the ache in my bruised heart and head, but that was it. Maybe I was blind, or closed-minded; maybe God and His peace, wisdom, and comfort were there, beneath the smoke and thumping bass. But I didn't have the strength to look for Him there. So I carried on, unchanged.

~

Hollywood is filled with hip spots and trendy clubs which, upon entering them, much like the church I attended that day, you will find music so loud you can't hear yourself think, much less anyone else speak. For a long time I've wondered why that is — why people would want to congregate at a place you can't even connect with each other. But through the years, I've come to realize the music that draws the crowds to these places is played loudly enough to drown out the chaos from their daily lives, allowing them to be with people without having to connect on any deeper level that might hurt too much.

Even outside of the clubs and churches, Hollywood is filled with deafening noises and distracting displays. They emanate through the thick air, taking their forms as sounds of traffic, pop music, conversations, billboards, flashing lights, and a neverending hurry to accomplish, capture, and be noticed. I was drawn to the dazzling lights and alluring beat of Los Angeles, but found the longer I existed in it, I stopped being able to hear and see both myself and God.

Our world now is filled with the chaotic noise of news, social media, and attempts to prove ourselves by accomplishing anything. But I think in the noise we have lost our ability to hear and see.

~

Lights from Downtown LA reflected off my face as I drove my little Ford Focus up and out of the Hollywood noise and into the hills, looking out over the endless grid of people stretching for miles. Climbing dark and winding roads, I drove as the light from the city faded behind me. The famous Mulholland Drive took me further and further from the chaos of the city and the chaos I had felt beating in my chest for weeks now. I pulled off at an outcropping, my tires skidding on the dirt as I brought my car, body, and mind to a halt and put them in park. I stepped out of my car, letting the door shut behind me as I walked to the edge of a striking cliff, perching me over all of Los Angeles. I stood there, still and silent, looking over the sparkling lights that stretched on into the dark, all the way to the ocean. I could see them, but they couldn't see me. It was there in the stillness I finally talked to God — I told Him my worries, my doubts, my hurt. A gentle wind blew across my face, and in it I heard the whispers of God's voice speaking gentle things into my heart. In the valley below, filled with its noise, quaking earth, and fiery glamor, I just couldn't hear Him. But here, above it all, in the quiet and gentle wind, I found Him, and He sat with me.

~

There's an ancient story about a prophet named Elijah who sought to bring salvation to a depraved and lost city, only to be attacked and forced to flee with just his life. In the midst of the noise of a lost city and the chaos of running for his life, Elijah falls into a deep despair, telling God to "take his life." It's there, deep inside his troubles, that God beckons Elijah up to a mountain to find His presence. When on the mountain and waiting for God to make Himself known, first there came a roaring storm with the power to break through rocks – but God was not in the storm. Then came a powerful earthquake, shaking the very ground Elijah stood upon – but God wasn't to be found in the earthquake. Then a mighty and terrifying fire appeared – but again, God was not found in the fire. Then, lastly, there appeared a gentle wind, and on it, a whisper – and it was there that the prophet found God.

~

We live in a time of storms, fires, and earthquakes. Often, in an attempt to drown the noise of this world out, we try to match it with our own. The nightclub-church was attempting to match the decibels of the noisy city in which it dwelt, in an effort to reveal God with its own noise. But I can't help feeling that perhaps God isn't interested in fighting for our attention like a desperate guy at a loud club. Perhaps instead, He invites us, like he did both me and Elijah, on a mountain into the quiet and still, away from the chaos of the world. Maybe it's there that we will finally be able to hear His still, small, but powerful voice.

Chapter 15

Bodies or Props

"Hollywood is a place where they'll pay you a thousand dollars for a kiss and fifty cents for your soul. I know, because I turned down the first offer often enough and held out for the fifty cents."
- Marilyn Monroe

One early smoggy September morning, I excitedly drove myself to a film set in the San Fernando Valley. I had booked a small role in a big film being made by an Oscar-winning director. I had nabbed the role because I could pull off a British accent, proving all those hours of watching the BBC and practicing my *'Ello guvna* in the mirror had paid off. It was a period film, so the wardrobe department put me in a turn of the century getup. Its heavy, itchy fabric immediately caused me to start sweating beneath the unforgiving California sun. But I didn't mind. I was just excited to be part of a "real" movie. We all were – me and the other few dayplayers that had been brought on to color the scenes.

I sat down in the actor holding area (no trailers for the small roles) next to a few of my comrades, who had also been draped in historical attire. We all greeted each other and talked excitedly about what parts we were playing. Across from me was a young woman. She seemed happy, but reserved, and perhaps a bit nervous – but excited. I smiled at her, and she smiled back. After a little while of talking more, a couple of the guys and I were taken to set to shoot our scene. The young woman hung back. Once placed on the set dressed up to look like a bar, I looked around and saw that the young woman who had been sitting with us still hadn't appeared on set. I leaned over to one of the other actors.

"Where is that girl we were hanging out with earlier?"

"Oh, she's doing a love scene with the main actor."

I nodded, understanding. Next door, while my bar scene was being shot, there was a closed set shooting what I later discovered was a very explicit "love" scene.

At lunch, we all gathered around the table again to recount how our days and scenes had been going. The girl, now dressed in a bathrobe, seemed quiet, more distant. She wasn't making eye contact like she had before. Something in her countenance had changed. I can't know for sure, but it seemed the excitement present just a few hours ago had been replaced with bits of shame and sadness in her eyes. I again smiled at her, and she meekly smiled back.

~

There's an enormous building on Ventura Blvd that I would pass every time I drove to auditions, right off Highway 101. On the top it had big bold letters, proudly advertising its company's presence and the things that went on inside its walls — it's the largest porn production company in the city. And every time I drove past it, I said a little prayer for anyone walking in, to combat the dark feeling that passed over me in the moments I was in its presence.

Los Angeles produces more pornography than anywhere else in the world. This is a fact I've heard repeated many times from many people, each knowing this shameful truth about the town. And it's true. I'm not surprised by this reality. Los Angeles is a world that sees humans as props, things to be used, taped, and spread out on magazines and billboards, then discarded. In the eyes of the entertainment industry, people aren't human, they're tools – tools used to titillate and exploit, then be gotten rid of when they no longer contain profitable characteristics. We tell ourselves this practice of using people and their bodies is empowering, that it's fine. It's not a big deal – it's just bodies, right? But are we *just* bodies?

Hollywood and most of modern culture no longer hold a view of the human person being anything more than a mass of cells. This view allows us to treat each other and others as disposable, because in a view of the human person, void of eternal perspective or intrinsic value, we are. This allows us to look at others as props, or tools, and objects to be used or sold, rather than people to be known and loved.

This reality is evidenced in the tragic life of people like Marilyn Monroe, whose story was recently told in the brutal and devastating biopic, *Blonde*. The film details Marilyn's story, played brilliantly by Ana De Armas, about a young girl with a deep desire to be loved, all the way through her adult life. That desire was exploited by countless people, men, and audiences who saw her only as an object to be used to lust after, make money from, and fantasize about, while ignoring the whole and valuable person beneath her skin. This tradition, of using and dehumanizing people (most often women) is age-old and has carried on to this day, detailed in a never ending line of tragic Hollywood stories we read about in the tabloids.

In 2006, a movement started called #MeToo, which sought to bring about justice for the abuse and dehumanizing behavior patterns that has seemed to plague Hollywood and culture at large for so long. It took over ten years for it to actually gain national attraction, and even then there was great pushback. It was a secular movement, and it's a good thing it happened. But part of me wishes it had been one started by people of faith, people who claim they believe humans have intrinsic value. But so often we preach one thing but practice the exact opposite.

I was once part of an acting class that was headed by a beloved acting teacher who self-described himself as "The Actor's Guardian Angel." This turned out to be a cruel irony, as his class was nothing but hell for those who joined believing it was a safe place in a preying city, instead finding it to be every bit as abusive and exploitative as every other wolf in sheep's clothing behind a producer's desk in Hollywood. Every week, he gave the more conventionally attractive women in the class roles for which they would have to disrobe or be in highly sexual situations with their scene partner. If they objected, he would tell them they couldn't ever be "real actors" unless they did, pressuring them until they gave in. One woman ended up walking off stage in tears, never coming back. Others were blamed for their own assaults, supposedly for leading men on. Others were ousted from the class for speaking up about abuse coming from the leadership. The teacher called the #MeToo movement "dangerous" for "taking down many good men," like the now infamous ones convicted of assault. In talking to many of the women who found themselves on the other end of these exploitative scenes, they expressed regret, anger, and shame in having been pushed and pressured to places they never wanted to go, ultimately angry that they had had their humanity stripped away.

There are many wolves in the world hungrily preying on the vulnerable in order to achieve power, pleasure, and position, at the expense of another's humanity. Even I, upon arriving in Hollywood and taking an odd job as an event staffer, was approached by a studio executive and asked to spend the night with them in return for being introduced to some movie stars at a party. I politely and dumbfoundedly declined the offer.

Unfortunately, stories like this are the norm. The stories of women I know who have been pressured, coerced, and goaded into places they wish they had never been are almost endless. And now, even the church-going guys of this generation are watching, taking part in, and defending the dehumanizing practice that the world normalized, on their computers, apps, and in real life, while turning around and raising their hands on Sunday morning.

I don't say this as some sort of sinless saint or holier-than-thou guy who's never messed up. I've struggled and failed at the often difficult task of choosing to see people like God does. I've objectified bodies for my own selfish pleasure. I've dehumanized people in my heart and mind to get what I want. But there's something that always pulls my gaze back to that of God's. It's the belief that every human, be it on a screen or in front of my face, isn't just a body to be used but a whole person, designed by a sentient creator, with eternal value. And even when I forget, even when I am tempted to objectify again, I see that young woman's face who I encountered on set all those years ago. She wasn't just a body, even though she had been hired as if she were. I see her sadness. I see her shame, and most of all I see her humanity. In seeing her and the countless people I know who have been used, chewed up, and spit out, I can't help but think of how Jesus looked at us, looks at me. Seeing us not as disposable objects, but as eternally whole, valuable people who bare his image.

Jesus exemplified this in every moment and interaction of his life, detailed in the Gospels. Every person who encountered him, even those who had been deemed worthless, left whole, with a new understanding of just how valuable they were. Jesus knelt in the dirt with the leper who had been cast out of society, healed him, and restored his humanity. Jesus sat with a "sinful woman" at a well and showed her her value beyond the reputation she carried. Jesus stepped in front of stones to rescue a woman who had made a mistake, lifted her off the ground, and offered her a new life. But he didn't stop there. He offers all of us, now, a knowledge of ourselves and others, beyond the objectification, dehumanization, and disposability we've both practiced and experienced.

Humans are not just props to be discarded, objects to buy, or bodies to objectify. God has created us in his image, carefully and beautifully with eternal value. May we grasp this truth and let it inform how we see and treat both ourselves and others who exist on screens, in Hollywood, on set, in class, in church, out of church, in front of us, and around us.

Chapter 16

The Escape Artists

"My soul is not contained within the limits of my body; my body is contained within the limitlessness of my soul."
- Jim Carrey

I had spent the last three days cooped up in my apartment in Hollywood. I lived in what used to be a famous hotel that had since been renovated and turned into a few hundred tiny studio apartments.

Sometimes I would lay on my couch (that also served as my bed) and imagine what old movie star might have stayed right there in my room: James Dean, Audrey Hepburn, or Cary Grant... I would envision the fabulous and exciting lives they led, and the fabulous things they might have experienced right where I was living. My imagination about their glamorous lives was juxtaposed by my own less-than-exciting life, as I lay sprawled out in my boxers, binge-watching yet another episode of something on my laptop to distract me from my boring life.

I was a few years into living in Los Angeles, and life hadn't turned into the vision that had played in my mind. I wanted to do something great, but it seemed that life didn't get the memo, and in the midst of a slowly creeping depression, I found myself spending days in my apartment, barely leaving, unless to get a cheap dinner from Subway.

Tired of being locked in my little cell of four whitewashed walls that I hadn't bothered to decorate, I got up off the couch, put on some pants, and walked out my door. I passed my neighbor, another actress-girl who always seemed to be coming home from her job at a local bar, and headed to the end of the long hall of tiny apartments filled with other people just like me, tired of waiting for their dreams to come true. At the end of the hall, I crawled out on the fire escape and began climbing until I reached the roof. There, I walked to the edge and sat down, my legs hanging off the edge of the tall building. I reached in my pocket and pulled out my pack of mini cigars. Lighting up, I breathed in. I let the smoke fall and spread across the vision before me. Below me, on the side of the building, was a billboard for a new blockbuster release, its lights shining up illuminating my face as I took another puff, the cherry at the end of the mini cigar burning bright as I inhaled.

From up on the roof, the city looked so small and manageable. The cars and people looked like the lego towns I built as a kid. I thought back to one of my favorite movies growing up, *The Truman Show*, a film about a man who unknowingly lives his whole life on a gigantic TV set, surrounded by actors, props, and unseen directors keeping him in a prison he doesn't know he's in. He's being watched by millions of people as he leads his exceedingly normal life, but the crux of the movie is when he begins to wonder if there's more. For an hour and a half, we watch Truman fight with everything he has to find the truth of what is really going on, assured that there has to be more. The thing is, Truman has everything he would need to be happy and comfortable – a wife, a job, a house – but somewhere in his heart of hearts, he knows there is more to life. The end of the movie finds Truman at a secret door he gives up everything to find, the door that leads to his freedom. It is evidence that his inclination that there was more was true. Right as he is about to leave everything he's ever known – certainty, comfort, the TV set – and walk through the door, Christoph, the director of The Truman Show, comes through a microphone like a voice of God, trying to convince Truman not to leave. He reminds Truman that there, in the fake TV show, Truman had everything he needed to be comfortable. It might be fake, but it was safe, predictable, understandable. You'll have to watch the movie to know what Truman decides. But as I sat there thinking about my life, for a second, I wondered if my life was a TV show. Maybe everything I did was a part of a reality show, and all the people I knew were actors, and the places I lived were sets. I laughed out loud, realizing my ridiculous and somewhat narcissistic thoughts. But in remembering *The Truman Show*, I couldn't help but feel a kinship with Truman. I often wondered why I couldn't just be happy with the comfort and predictability I had. I wondered why I was cursed to want more, to have this need to chase dreams and ask questions. I saw so many other people around me accepting their cells of safety and predictability. Why couldn't I? And some good it was doing me – here I was, nowhere close to the "more" I thought I'd find on my journey. Like Truman, I was stuck in my cell of a small apartment and unlived dreams, but cursed with the unshakable belief that there was more. I took one more pull off the cigar and flicked the final embers off the side of the building, watching them fall and disappear into the night. I looked out one more time, still with this belief I was made for more, but unsure how to find it, before I climbed back down into my room and closed the door.

~

As I look at the world around me, and even my own small world, I see so many of us living in cells. No, they're not covered with bars, or surrounded by concrete walls – they're much more comfortable and hard to see. In fact, many of us don't even know they're cells at all. Like Truman, we are trapped in cages of comfort, safety, and routine that have lulled to sleep the cry in our hearts that says there's more. We have traded true and lifelong committed romance for the cell of easy hookups and dating apps. We have traded living a life of meaning and purpose for the pursuit of money and status. We have traded a deep, centered faith and relationship with God for the promises of politicians and our own invented truth. But there, beneath the comfort of a modern world that offers us such well-marketed cells, is the cry for more — a cry that beckons us to search beyond the trappings of this world to the eternal things that our soul truly longs for, the things that stretch into a world beyond what we can see. Though our cells are safe, they are not where we were made to live.

Chapter 17

Applause, Awards, & Adoration

"If you come to fame not understanding who you are, it will define who you are."
- Oprah Winfrey

I held my breath as the curtains parted. A hot spotlight shone down on me as I squinted my eyes past its blinding rays to the audience of hundreds, seated expectantly in the large hall. In my sweaty hands, I held three large metal rings; concealed in my pocket were red scarves; hidden on my wrist beneath my sleeve was a lighter with flash paper, loaded into a secret compartment, ready to go. Suddenly the music began, and so did I. I linked the rings, made the scarves appear with a flourish, and for the big finale, lit a flash of fire into the dark theater. The music stopped. Then, applause — lots of applause. Some people were standing, some were cheering. I was bowing. This was my first real taste of the addicting and alluring draw of performing. It came with such a powerful hit of adoration. It was just magic camp, and I was just fourteen, but it was intoxicating, and I wanted more.

A few years later, I captured that feeling again on the stage of my high school during the much-anticipated "Battle of the Bands." Our now-infamous band, The Summertime Cherubs, was comprised of my best friends, Matt, Ben, and Chad playing guitar, drums, and piano, respectively — and me, standing front and center, taking the role of lead singer. Dressed in white jeans and a white shirt, complete with platinum blond hair, I belted our original tunes to the crowd of my peers. When the final emo, alternative, Disney-esque note faded into the night, suddenly, again, I felt the hit of adrenaline as the school theater burst into applause.

A few years later, I sat in an AMC theater in Los Angeles, surrounded by a room full of excited people at the premiere of a film I was in. I felt a nervous excitement as the lights dimmed and I watched my image live on the screen. I felt the rush of gratification both in doing what I loved, and being seen doing it by people who liked it. The same familiar hit of satisfaction coursed through my body as the credits rolled to the sound of applause, while my name appeared on screen.

~

Applause is powerful. One might think it's only an addiction for the actors, singers, and dancers of the world. But it is powerful to performers — and we each, in our own way, are performers. From the time we are children, we learn to crave the doting praise of our parents, as we hold up crudely-colored pictures in hopes of its presentation on the refrigerator door. This desire for adoration weaves its way through our entire lives, from adolescence with the desire to sit at the cool kids table, all the way through to adulthood, hoping to find adoration for our performances in grades, degrees, promotions, and awards. Social media was an invention that strikes directly to the human need to be loved for the lives we live and the things we do, giving us a dopamine hit with every like, heart, comment, or view we rack up. But it's never enough.

Many have tried to solve this problem by simply attempting to will ourselves to not care. In some self-help books and religious philosophies, the "answer" to the unquenchable need for adoration lies in simply pretending we don't have the need. Others have tried to answer it by putting all of their hope for adoration in romantic relationships, but ultimately find no one person can fulfill the insatiable thirst we have for love. And others, still, live as if they don't need anyone at all, but eventually find, after years of isolation, a toxic bitterness has grown, and eats away at their soul like a cancer. And some spend their entire lives trying to earn adoration through their work and performance, only to find themselves tired and never full. In the end, the deep longing inside each of our hearts will push us past whatever pop-philosophy, personal determination, or imperfect relationship can offer, back into the neverending search for a love outside ourselves.

We were created to be adored by an infinite and unwavering affection that we simply cannot find in any sort of lasting fullness on this earth. Which leads me to believe that if we were created to desire something so deeply that we can find nowhere in this universe, perhaps the fulfillment of this desire lies beyond it.

God offers us this love. God offers us this attention. God offers us this adoration. And what might be scariest of all is, we can do nothing to earn, find, or deserve it. There's no show we can put on, no moral work we can do, and no problem we can solve to get it. We are already given it. Not because of anything we have done, but instead because of who He is. But living with the knowledge and letting it change us is easier said than done.

The "likes," adoration, and rewards of this world can seem so much more visceral than the ones from an unseen God. But ultimately, as we inevitably see, they are so much more fleeting and so much less filling. When I perform and receive applause, the high of the adoration satiates me for an hour before I find myself hungrier than ever before.

Every year in Hollywood, there's a time of year called "Awards Season." It's a time when all the beautiful, talented, and rich stars of the entertainment industry throw lavish parties and hold ceremonies to celebrate the movies, shows, films, and productions of the past year. While it takes place in Hollywood, the season echoes around the world, as the excitement of the glamorous lives and large awards, things we all long for are put on display in envy-inducing shows. Something about this season strikes to the very heart of what we each want.

For many years, I have watched the pageantry with friends at Oscar parties held in small Los Angeles apartments, all the while egotistically protesting, saying I didn't "really care" about awards, and snarkily commenting through the multi-hour-long program. But in my heart of hearts, I would be lying if I said there wasn't a twinge of jealousy flowing through my soul as I watched the adoration these stars had poured upon them.

Through the years, in acting classes, student film sets, and late-night apartment conversations, I've heard countless young actors talk about what they will do "when" they win their Oscar. I had one friend who had already written his acceptance speech. Condescendingly, I've laughed at their unrealistic dreams and lauded myself for being a more realistic, truer artist, dedicated to the form, not the accolades. But in the interest of honesty, in my silent times, when no one can see, I've spent countless hours lying in my bed, looking up and into the dark of my room, imagining myself on that stage, accepting my Academy Award, imagining the things I would say while holding that little golden statue.

I've heard pastors and online prophets call the Oscar Award ceremony a sign of human selfishness, and the small golden statue an obvious, and somewhat unsubtle, image of a modern idol. I don't entirely disagree. But what I have realized is that almost every idol, both found in scripture or in the modern world, is the imagined fulfillment of a deeply human need in a destructive way that ultimately leads to ruin.

We each were created to be seen, loved, and adored, in some way, shape, or form. For some of us, that form is in a golden statue, for others, it might look like something else. But why? Why do we need this? Why did God create us with this need to be adored? And why does adoration feel so good? I think, perhaps, it's because when we are adored, we are assured there is something good about who we are. And in the depths of our hearts, we need to know that we, or at least something about ourselves, is good. So in this desperate need, we look to be assured of that from golden statues, promotions, awards, or relationships, and some of us stop looking for that and simply find escape.

But we have been told there is something good in us. We have been told we are valuable. And we have been told we are loved. But this love, from God, is one that will not tarnish. It will not fade, and it can't be taken away from us. So now the question becomes not, "Should I desire love and adoration?" and instead becomes, "Where will I find it, and is it a true, lasting, and ultimately a fulfilling love and adoration?"

Chapter 18

Bo

"Life, to me, doesn't feel like a straightforward story; it doesn't make sense for me to get up there and just tell a story. Life feels like what my show feels like: chaotic and strange and disconnected. "
- Bo Burnham

There's a guy named Bo. Bo is an actor and writer like me. Bo moved to Hollywood about the same time I did. Bo is tall, blonde, and lanky like I am. Bo is funny and philosophical like people tell me I am. Bo started off making little movies on his phone when he was a teen, just like I did.

Unlike me, Bo is now rich and famous.

Recently my acting agent told me a very large movie studio wanted me to audition for a lead role in their next project. This was the biggest audition I had ever received. Up until this point, I had only ever been cast in small, somewhat meaningless bit parts, with a line here and a fleeting reaction shot there. But now, I was being considered for a leading role, one that actually mattered. So I excitedly prepared my lines, carefully recorded my audition, and hopefully sent it in. Then, I waited, and waited, and waited... every day, hoping to hear that I had landed the big part. But I never got that call. I never got any call. Instead, one morning I opened the digital paper on my phone and saw a headline telling me that Bo had been cast in the role I had auditioned for.

When I heard the news that Bo had been cast and I had not, I felt the same ache I had felt when I was fourteen and hadn't gotten the lead in a summer camp play, and instead was given a pity role with one line – the ache that informed me that I didn't really matter all that much. But it wasn't just a movie or play I didn't get cast in, it was something much bigger. Bo hadn't just been cast in the movie I wanted to be in. Bo had been cast in the life I desperately wanted to live – one where he mattered, where who he was and what he did was important, where he was a compelling lead character, telling a great story.

I actually like Bo. I think he's smart and funny, and I have a feeling that if we ever hung out, we'd get along. But I'd be lying if I said there isn't just an occasional wave of, "Why not me?" that hits me in the gut when I see our similarities, then look at the great story he gets to tell and the lead character he gets to play inside it. This is because, it turns out, the resentment I feel has almost nothing to do with Bo or the life he leads, but instead it has to do with me and the life I wish I had, one where I was a lead character.

~

I Google myself more often than I'd like to admit. I tell anyone who might catch me doing this that I'm just, "making sure the information is correct," but truth be told, as I scroll through my links, bio, work, and pictures, I'm looking for evidence that will assure me that I'm someone with significance, evidence that will tell me that my story matters. That *I* matter.

At the core of every human heart lies the immovable desire to live as a main character in a great story, because the main characters of great stories are meaningful, compelling, significant, and loved. We know this to be true because every single movie we've ever seen has told us it is. We only get a little bit of time on this earth to find that significance, which is the conduit to receiving what we were made to desire. But while we each dream of being cast as the leading men and women of great stories, we believe that unfortunately, we didn't get the role — Bo did.

We all have a Bo. Maybe they're not a famous actor or a rock star; maybe they're someone whose books we read, whose church we go to, whose Instagram we follow — but we all have a Bo. Even Bo has a Bo; someone who is like us, but unlike us, who is acting out a role in a life we can only dream of being cast in. When confronted with their significance and value in relation to our insignificance and obscurity, we say things to make ourselves feel better, like, "They were just at the right place at the right time," or, "I wouldn't even want what they have!" or, "They're probably a bad person in real life." But deep down, in the secret places of our hearts, we question why they were cast and we weren't.

There's a phrase the kids are throwing around on TikTok: *main character energy*. It's a title generally bestowed on someone with a big personality, who's funny, charming, and interesting. "Main character energy" is now used to describe someone who has traits that resemble the protagonists in our favorite movies: charm, influence, and adoration, all of which add up to importance – all the markings of someone who matters enough to be cast as a lead in the movie of life we're all trying out for. But now it's being applied to unscripted people in real life, which potentially could be a scary thing. Here in "real life," like movies, we believe there are a limited number of "lead roles" that will inevitably go to the most handsome and charismatic stars, the rest of us "normies" being relegated to living the lives of extras, just blurs in the background of other people's important and meaningful movies.

The reality is, the world is just high school, but on a bigger level — each of us judging the importance of ourselves, our stories, and our significance based on the table we find ourselves sitting at. We all wish we were sitting with the jocks and cheerleaders, living gossip-worthy lives, but most of us have to come to grips with the reality that we're actually at the loser table, where all the other "normal" people sit, with our mortgages, difficult marriages, mundane jobs, and meaningless lives. It's hard not to look at the surrounding tables and imagine how much better it must be "over there," living the lives of prom queens and quarterbacks who get to live out stories of catching touchdowns and making out in cars. I often find myself sitting at my table and looking at Bo's — filled with other smart, funny, and pretty people in the middle of the room, each holding awards, dressed in "likes," and making plans for their weekend parties I won't be at — and I wonder why I haven't been invited to sit there. Am I not talented, smart, or interesting enough? Am I not main character material?

~

We all play roles in the movie called life — just not the ones we wished we did. Most of us feel we have been cast in roles that we deem boring and meaningless, roles like: employee, parent, dropout, has-been, or never-was. A lot of books, studies, and articles say that due to social media, magazines, and TV, we're facing a "contentment and comparison" problem that's affecting our self-worth as a result of measuring our value according to the metrics of money, popularity, beauty, talent, and intelligence. I think they're *almost* right. I think instead, we measure our self-worth by the metrics of story. We use those things as identifying markers for ourselves and others to determine who gets to play what role in the story of life. Essentially, we see life as the movie and we link our personal value to the quality of our roles in it. And most of us feel we just didn't get a very important part. It was never about what Bo had — it was about what I didn't.

Today, it's almost impossible to escape the game of comparing our lives to others, with our constant engagement with TV, magazines, and movies. There's literally a feature on Instagram called "stories" where you can tap through endless accounts of everyone else's great/exciting/meaningful life — evidenced by their fitter bodies, nicer houses, deeper pockets, happier relationships, higher education, better morals, further travels, cooler parties, and bigger followings that underline the reality that they are main characters, and we are not. If you looked at my Instagram feed, you'd find pictures of me doing really cool things, in really cool places, with really cool people, with really cool lighting. You might even find yourself thinking that I'm a main character, because if I'm honest, that's what I want you to think about me — because that's what I want to think about me. But all those "cool" things are just blips inside a very normal life that so often feels meaningless. If you could see past the "main character" pictures I post, you'd see me, on my couch, in my little apartment, on my phone, looking at Bo's profile, thinking the same thing about him and his life.

There's a saying going around now that goes something like, "Don't compare your behind-the-scenes to everyone else's highlight reels." I think that there just might be some wisdom hidden inside of this seemingly obvious bit of insta-piration

~

In 2020, a worldwide pandemic changed and rocked the world in a way where every last person on the face of the earth was affected. It was a terrible event that stopped short (some, sadly, permanently) every story on the face of the earth, big or small, significant or obscure. A universal "pause" button had been pressed, and every life on the face of the earth came to a screeching halt. I suddenly found myself unable to pursue, attempt, or do the things that brought me that feeling of significance I so desired. I couldn't act in or make movies, travel, or further the story I was trying to tell. So, in the throes of an uncertain future and an affectless present, I sunk into a depression that filled me with questions about who I was, and what I was worth if I wasn't able to chase a story I deemed meaningful.

So, I did what everyone else did; I laid in bed, read books, and watched TV to distract myself. I mostly watched reruns of old and comforting shows, as all film and TV production shut down and very little new entertainment was being released. But one day, as I lazily scrolled through Netflix, hoping to distract myself with some mindless entertainment, I saw that Bo had released a new comedy/musical special called *Inside*, that he had filmed during his time in the lockdown.

The special was still classic Bo – funny, smart, etc. But this time, there was something different that had only appeared in flashes of his older specials: painful, authentic humanity. This time, there was no live audience of thousands of adoring fans laughing and applauding at every joke, instead there were just blank whitewashed walls around him. This time, there was no stage with red curtains or giant screens, instead he performed his special in a small, empty room. This time, the routine wasn't a string of quippy and clever upbeat bits, but instead was a collection of honest, sometimes heartbreaking songs that made him look less like the "main character" I had made him out to be in my mind and more like a fellow human detailing his own longing for significance, desire for purpose, bitterness at coming up empty, and disillusionment with a world that felt (at the time) anything but meaningful. As the credits rolled, I suddenly felt my perception of myself, Bo, and the stories we were living out, change. He was no longer some charming leading man who lived on a screen. Instead, he was a person who was struggling with the exact same things I was. My insecurity and resentment for him and his life faded, and the feelings of connection and a shared human experience took their place. This connection and discovery was only possible because Bo was brave enough as an artist and human to remove his glossy celebrity façade and show the flawed but even more beautiful human beneath it. A human who, like me, was reaching for the infinite and everlasting story.

~

It's interesting to see how God incarnated into the world. For centuries, as God's people awaited His coming on earth, they pictured how it would look when He showed up. They imagined he would arrive in epic movie fashion, as a mighty king costumed in robes, onto a mighty throne in the hills, wielding his celebrity power over the world. But when God did step into our reality, He came as a baby, wrapped in cloth, laying in an animal feeding trough. He grew up in a normal working class family. He worked as a craftsman. He hung out with common people. He preached in fields to anyone who would listen. He died alone on a cross. Not really the blockbuster movie people had been expecting the God of the universe to cast Himself in. This is because God has a very different idea of what makes a lead character and meaningful story — found in his Sermon on the Mount.

"God blesses those who are poor and realize their need for him,
    for the Kingdom of Heaven is theirs.
God blesses those who mourn,
    for they will be comforted.
God blesses those who are humble,
    for they will inherit the whole earth.
God blesses those who hunger and thirst for justice,
    for they will be satisfied.

God blesses those who are merciful,

>   for they will be shown mercy.

God blesses those whose hearts are pure,

>   for they will see God.

God blesses those who work for peace,

>   for they will be called the children of God.

God blesses those who are persecuted for doing right,

>   for the Kingdom of Heaven is theirs."

The entire sermon is about who Jesus is interested in casting in the story he's telling, referred to as, "The Kingdom of Heaven," which is the most important story that could ever be told — one about the redemption of the entire universe. And as it turns out, there are leading parts for all of us. But the skills, talents, and experience needed for the lead roles are very different from the ones we as humans value in the stories we're telling. I've never seen a Hollywood casting notice for, "needs to be poor and know it," or, "has to have been humbled," or, "someone who has experienced mourning." But it seems these are the characteristics that Jesus looks for in his leading men and women — and the good news is, I don't know anyone who doesn't have these on their resume.

God, the great storyteller, has written into our very hearts the desire to be cast as a main characters in a meaningful story – ultimately, the one He is telling. And you and I have been invited to play leading roles in the most important movie that will ever be made.

~

I will almost assuredly never be as popular, successful, talented, or funny as Bo. But perhaps I don't need to be to tell a beautiful, meaningful, and significant story. Maybe if I act in the likeness of the God who created stories, I will find one actually worth living in, being a part of, in even a small way, building the everlasting Kingdom of Heaven – by loving the people around me, noticing the beauty in the world, doing what I love, and knowing Him. These are all the things that add up to me becoming a compelling leading man in a truly meaningful story – one that I have already been cast into, should I only read my lines.

I'm still going to watch Bo's specials and wish it was me up there on that screen. I might still feel a twinge of envy when he wins an Emmy (I already did when he did), and a touch of jealousy when he is cast in movies and I am not. But I'm going to try to remember that a lead role in a significant life is available to me right here, right now.

Chapter 19

Cheesy is Beautiful

"Continue to share your heart with people even if it's been broken."
- Amy Poehler

I took my seat in the middle of a giant IMAX theater. People trickled one by one into the room with popcorn and hushed smiles, like me, ready to escape into a summer movie for a couple of hours. It was a musical, just the thing I needed to cleanse my palate from a long and difficult pandemic year and a half. Right before the movie began, a mom, dad, and their teenage son scooted past me and found their chairs. The teenager plunked himself down next to me, sprawling his gangly body over his seat, visibly uncomfortable to be at a movie with his parents that would certainly be deemed uncool by high school boys.

The movie began with a catchy and angsty song about feeling lonely and separated from the world and immediately I was hooked. As the story unfolded in dramatic dialogue, evocative shots, and emotional musical and acting performances, I was more and more pulled into the coming-of-age tale. I looked to my right, down my row of friends, and saw them each engrossed in the youthful but timeless story of wanting to be loved and seen. All of us fully grown adults, we were each aware and touched by this musical that spoke to the heart of what it means to be human, in a sweet, heartstrings-pulling, perhaps even sappy way — a way that invited us to a place where our desire for the beautiful things in life was encouraged, and understanding for the difficulty of life was validated in overly but perfectly dramatic musical numbers.

I'm not typically someone who tears up at movies and have even been made fun of for my more stoic approach to viewing art. But even I found myself a bit misty during a scene where the protagonist, who struggled with severe mental illness and anxiety (something I've lived with my entire life), falls down on a stage after fumbling his words in front of all his peers, only to rise and sing a beautiful and rousing song about being found, and not alone. But in the middle of the song, as I was attempting to keep tears from my eyes, I heard a scoff next to me. I stole a glance to my left where the gangly teen was sitting. He had a countenance of contempt and condescension as the character on screen emotionally sang his heart out. I grinned, remembering my time as an adolescent youth, desperate to be cool (much like the character in the movie). I noticed throughout the remainder of the film, at every emotionally resonant scene, another scoff or moan would make itself known by my teenage row-mate. The movie carried on, pulling heartstrings more and more, and eventually my adolescent friend pulled his hood up and over his head, sinking lower in his seat, undoubtedly in an attempt to put distance between him, a cool teen and the sweet, even cheesy, movie before him.

After the movie had ended and I had wiped my eyes dry, I walked out of the theater with a renewed feeling of hope, and a fresh belief in the goodness that still lay at the heart of life. But it turns out, not everyone felt the way I did. Upon looking at the reviews for the film, I found that it was almost unanimously hated by all of the most important film critics, each citing similar reasons to dislike the musical. The most famous reviewer summed up their collective opinions by stating that this coming-of-age high school story about longing to be seen was ultimately just "emotionally manipulative" and "cloying." I was surprised at how different our experiences had been, and perhaps even more surprised at the vitriol this unassuming, sweet, film had garnered from these reviewers. But then I thought back to the teenager in the seat beside me during the movie. I remembered his scoffs, and how perfectly, even predictably, they came on cue at any moment in the film that became emotional, sweet, beautiful, or authentic.

In reading the dismissive, condescending, and even mean-spirited reviews of this film, I realized that these reviewers, and perhaps many of us have, in the wake of terrible times and broken lives, allowed ourselves to stop believing the world can be beautiful. We attempt to stop wanting what we worry might not exist – and fear if it does, we don't have a place inside it, because *we* don't feel beautiful. So we become hardened, making only and praising only art made with snark and cynicism that tells us whatever beauty you see is a lie and isn't real or lasting, and the only way to make it through this life is to let out nihilistic laughs to drown out the sound of gentle authenticity beckoning us towards goodness. And so, sincerity is mocked or ignored like we would a man on the corner talking about heaven. Because so far, all we've experienced is hell. To believe there could be more is not only scary, but painful, as it reveals how far from who we should or could be.

We're not brave enough to believe the world could be beautiful. If we did, we might have to come face to face with the reality that we were wrong, and we were idiots for believing it could be, that we were stupid for longing for that to begin with. So we must deny a central part of our humanity – namely, the desire for goodness, beauty, and hope, so as to not be made fools of by a world so often cruel, chaotic, and mean. In our powerlessness to defeat the negativism of existence, we take a, "if you can't beat it, join it," stance to protect ourselves from a broken universe. So we pull up our hoods to separate ourselves from the beauty of life and scoff like a teenage bully at those who reach for it, because we are not strong enough to believe, much less bear, the goodness in the world.

But what if we were made for beauty? What if we were designed to desire goodness, authenticity, sincerity, and hope, and the self-protecting cynicism we employ is actually keeping us from experiencing heaven? Yes, life is difficult. But the ones who, like the main character of the film, believe there is still goodness in the world, even in the face of bad reviews and adolescent scoffs, will be the ones who find it.

Chapter 20

The Characters We Play

"I'm curious about other people. That's the essence of my acting. I'm interested in what it would be like to be you."
- Meryl Streep

I've been a psychopath, a high school jock, a college nerd, a mental ward patient, a doctor, a pastor, a frat boy, a cop, a cowboy, an intern, a vigilante, a cult member, a robber, a boy band member, a biker thug, a soldier, a guy next door... and that's just on screen.

I always enjoyed getting fit for costumes. Entering the wardrobe houses deep in the valley was a magical experience, walking by rows and rows of props, wardrobe pieces, and outfits worn in beloved movies, filling the musty air with smells of Febreze and cinema history. Room after room, I passed the objects and clothes that brought to life the worlds they inhabited. In the dressing room, I would stand in my underwear, being gazed at by the wardrobe department as they slowly but surely placed items on my body. Piece by piece, cloth by cloth, they built a new character using my frame as the canvas. With every piece of clothing, hat, prop gun, pair of shoes, belt, jewelry, or fake tattoo that was placed on me, little by little, I disappeared and a new totally other character emerged, until finally, with the finishing touches, Nathan had ceased to exist in the wake of the new character that was built and could live and breathe on screen and in a story.

I remember watching hours of a TV show as a kid called *Reading Rainbow*, with a guy named Levar Burton. Levar had a passion for helping kids love to read and learn through the art of stories. I had seen every episode, but there was one episode that became my favorite – the one I demanded my mom put on again and again. It was the one where Levar walked through a crazy hat store, with every kind of cap you can imagine. Every hat he put on took him to another world. He would put on a pirate hat and suddenly he'd be on the sea; he'd put on an astronaut's helmet and then be exploring the wonders of space; he'd put on a construction helmet and then be building a skyscraper. Every time the episode would end, I'd think about what it would be like to be in that hat store, and imagine all the wonderful characters I could become.

As a kid, I spent my days and free hours inhabiting other worlds as fantastical characters that looked like the ones I would see on screens and read about in books. I learned how to act out these characters, even if just for myself in my room and backyard. I learned their mannerisms, their worldview, and how to turn myself into who they were. I loved playing characters. It allowed me to become something greater than myself, to be a part of something bigger, to be stronger than I actually was. I became the characters I either wanted or needed to be.

When I would play video games or read books, I would spend hours setting my character, either in my mind or on the screen, to look just like me so I could imagine myself as the one exploring worlds, conquering foes, and wooing fair maidens.

When I became an adult, I didn't want to stop playing pretend, dressing up, or becoming characters, so I made a career out of it. I became an actor. For at least a few days a month, I could live out, even imaginarly, an enticing story and play an interesting character.

For the longest time, I believed that playing characters was just my job – that it was something I did on screen for a time. Then the director would yell cut, I would take off my costume, cash my check, and I would stop acting out the character... or so I thought. Not long ago, after a particularly hard season, I sat on a couch talking to my therapist. I told him I didn't like the person I was becoming, that the choices I was making felt like a different person. He then told me about the psychological concept of people creating multiple versions of themselves at different times in their life for different purposes. I thought about it, and he was right – when I was insecure, I became an insecure, chubby, nerd Nathan that wanted to sit at the cool kids table; when I was angry, I became a hulking jerk; when I was depressed, I became a nihilistic loner in a leather jacket smoking a cigarette. On and on, we explored these characters I had unintentionally created through the twists and turns of my story throughout my life. Most of these characters were made when I was very young, and he told me they were cast for a purpose, often for protection, safety, the need to feel valuable, or to deal with trauma. But he also told me that to live a healthy life, I had to choose and create who I actually wanted to be. I had to decide which and what character was beneficial to the life I wanted to lead, to the story I wanted to tell.

~

We all drag around a rucksack of characters. I see it both in myself and the people around me. Some of them are egocentric, to hide from their insecurities; some of them are victims, unable to find agency in the world; some of them are the bad guys, telling us to take what we want and need, no matter the cost. Dressing up in costumes in our mind, each of these characters come to life as we cast them in the scenes of our lives, choosing which character will get us closest to the ending we desire, or at least protect us until the director yells "Cut!" But what we don't often realize is that when we cast these different versions of ourselves in the scenes of our lives, these characters and the choices they make are shaping, little by little or sometimes in one terrible moment, what kind of story we are telling.

So many of us have this idea that we are just one monolithic person. We take personality tests like the Enneagram, Myers-Briggs, and read horoscopes to be told exactly who we are. We do this in an effort to know who we are, or perhaps who we should be. Living in Hollywood, I quickly found that it was a city and industry filled with people searching for an identity. Lost in a sea of chaos, confusing voices, and a cast full of different characters, young people come from around the world to find themselves in a very dark city that's ready to sweetly lie to them so as to use them for its own gains. Very often, after having met aspiring actors, I find they have very little interest in acting, but an aching desire to be considered an actor – their desire not being found in learning and practicing a craft, but instead finding themselves adored and validated from a life in the spotlight. They just wanted to wear the actor hat. But the spotlight is illusive and selective, and after a few years of trying to get its attention, many of these "actors" find themselves even more empty and tired than before after not being cast as the "star."

Both Hollywood and personality tests promise to tell us exactly who we are in return for something – either fifteen minutes online checking boxes, or a life desperately chasing an unreachable "dream." But even if they give us an answer, it can only ever be a small part, an incomplete picture of who we really are. The reality is, we are a jumble of multiple archetypes that make appearances in different scenes in our lives, depending on the circumstances and stage directions.

Living with all these characters fighting to take over in different scenes and seasons of our lives can sometimes feel like we are being ripped apart at the seams. It can feel like we will never know who we actually are, and what kind of story we are telling. God came into our world to fix that. A great philosopher by the name of Saint Paul wrote about this in a book called 1 Thessalonians saying:

"May God himself, the God who makes everything holy and whole, make you holy and whole, put you together—spirit, soul, and body—and keep you fit for the coming of our Master, Jesus Christ. The One who called you is completely dependable. If he said it, he'll do it!"

We're all playing dress up, putting on the costumes we choose, and some that have been forced upon us in order to make us feel and look stronger, more in charge, and more confident than we really are. But God stepped into our world to un-fracture us, to vanquish each of these personas we've created and to help us discover who we truly are. Like the costumers who placed clothes upon my body to help me become a different character, God comes and gently strips all of the costumes off of us, layer by layer, until the character is gone and only we remain. He starts with the shirt, then the pants, the jacket, and the shoes; he washes our feet, rubs the product out of our hair, and slowly destroys all of the characters we've created, so we can finally be who He made us to be.

Without Him, we needed these characters. But with Him, we are free to be ourselves. We no longer have to play the role of the tough guy — His presence will protect us. We no longer have to play the role of victim — His power will empower us. We no longer have to play the role of bad guy — His grace will give us everything we need. With Him next to us, we are free to fire all of the characters we've been employing and cast our true selves in the story of our lives. With Him in charge as the director, we need not fear we won't know our lines. He is there every step, flub, and falter to help us through each scene. And with every take, we get better, not at playing a character, but living as ourselves.

What characters have you created? What personas have you cast in the story of your life? Were they born in times of fear, uncertainty, or chaos? What do they look like? Why did you feel the need to create them? And what are the scenes where you feel them come out? But most importantly, the question we all must ask is, when God takes off the costume, who are we really?

Chapter 21

Acting Like God

"Life beats you down and crushes the soul and art reminds you that you have one."
- Stella Adler

My talent manager Lou and I stepped into a bustling theater. We maneuvered our way to the will-call window, then pushed through an anxious crowd towards our seats. The usher helped us to our section, where we scooted along a packed row in the balcony to the very center — best seat in the house. Sitting down and stuffing our jackets on the floor beneath our chairs, we looked up, took a breath, and gazed out over the grand old hall, gilded with century-old wall carvings, Renaissance-style paintings, and lights guiding our eyes to the stage that stood empty, eagerly awaiting the actor's arrival, who would be telling a story upon it. We were here because Lou had scored us tickets to see one of my very favorite actors doing a live performance of a beloved play. Adam would soon be appearing in person, on stage, and the whole room was emanating a subdued excitement. The lights dimmed and the dull murmurs immediately stopped as we all waited, with bated breath, to see this star arrive.

It was an old play written many decades ago. It was about family and loss, death and love, triumph and pain – the human stuff. And from the second Adam appeared on stage, the whole room was transfixed. With grace and human grit, Adam gave a performance that would stun even the hardest of hearts. Every second he performed, he made it impossible to look away. Thousands of eyes were fixed on his brutally honest performance that touched each of us in a unique way. The whole play was beautiful, but there was one scene that still plays in my mind. Adam's character, an egocentric, blustering playboy, is suddenly struck with the pain of being alone. Dropping to the ground, he lifted his head to heaven and let out a cry before burying his head in his hands and sobbing. It was heart-wrenching, it was beautiful, and it was me. Lately, I had been working through my own unhealed wounds that had reared their ugly heads. And like the strong man I was, I ignored and pushed it down so as not to deal with the fallout, should it bubble over and ruin my frantic attempts to keep the seas of hurt at bay. I wanted to express and process my pain. I wanted to cry, to scream, but I couldn't. But as I watched Adam's character on stage, I was suddenly allowed to take part in the cathartic process that story provided us. This character became the personification of my own experience, and through Adam's performance, I was offered a bit of healing as a result. Chills traveled across my skin as I watched Adam take his performance to a place that was so real I was able to feel my own pain through his acting. I was able to cry not only for the hurts and pain in this character's life, but my own. Adam took on my pain, and the pain of everyone in that room, when he allowed himself to enter the fully human experience of this story.

As Lou and I left that day, my problems weren't fixed. My depression hadn't simply vanished, and I still had the same foes facing me as when I had walked in. But for a moment, I was able to, through a compelling story and an authentic performance, find just a small bit of healing, as Adam had taken on the pain I couldn't feel and felt it for me on stage. Like a metaphorical transference of pain, I was able to let the deep and bruised places in my soul be healed through another's willingness to hold my, and everyone else's, hurt. This is why good acting is so powerful.

~

All the great acting teachers throughout history have ultimately all come to the same conclusion: for a performance to be good, it must be real. Only then will the audience be able to connect their own human experience to it. When an actor allows themselves to be fully human, raw, and real, it offers the audience a chance to take part in the character on the stage or the screen's process of healing so that we can find even just a bit of healing in our own lives. Art has a powerful ability to help us translate and transfer our lived experience and make sense of it. Good art, stories, songs, and movies help us process our own deeply human experiences in the context of a story, make sense of it through deep catharsis, and let us know we aren't alone in our very human journeys. A good acting performance allows us to cast all our pain, hurt, desire, and hope on it, and in return, it can turn it into something beautiful. But these performances aren't cheap. There's a reason they are so few and far between. These roles cost. We have all heard the stories of an actor getting so lost in a role they go crazy — some ending up on drugs, in mental wards, or even dying. To act in a role so powerful that it has the ability for people to cast their humanity upon it, it must be anchored in the deep but painful reality of life. But in an act of sacrificial love for the viewer, the actor offers themselves, their dignity, and their pride so their performance can be used to make us more beautiful.

~

When an actor offers themselves up and sacrifices themselves in a role for the healing and catharsis of others, they are acting in the direct example of Jesus, who did this for real, for the entire world. As actors take on the sadness, pain, and hurt of those watching them in a movie, they do it in the same way Jesus did on the cross. Jesus gave us the true example of what it means to bear the burden of another's pain at his own expense. Actors on screen bear the weight of pain from every single person watching them. They embody the human experience for the viewer, taking all the shame, hurt, embarrassment, loss, and grief that every person watching has ever experienced. And like Jesus bearing the weight of the world's hurt, take it off the viewer and heave it onto their own shoulders, so that for just a moment, the audience can be free.

When we watch actors in a painful scene, we don't watch them experience just their own pain – we watch them experience ours, collectively. In this way, art heals us. It heals us temporarily in the same way the God of the universe heals us eternally – by taking every mistake, regret, and hurtful memory upon himself and to death so that we can live.

So don't turn from sad scenes, don't hide your eyes when you feel like crying, and don't look away when confronted with the catharsis God has displayed for the whole world to see – for you to see.

Chapter 22
Christian Movies?

"Life goes on. People pass along. Nothing stays the same. The Lord gives and The Lord takes away. That's the way He is."
- Terrence Malick

I nervously pressed "send" and as the email wooshed to a major media outlet, carrying with it the words of an article I had written entitled, "Why I Won't Make Another Christian Film," I felt both the fear of certain change and the excitement for a new and unknown adventure.

I had made three feature length Christian movies. After the success of my first film, made from my first script — the one I had, by faith, put together in my old apartment — I was able to begin making more and more movies. They were modern interpretations of

Bible stories, and every time I released a new film, the same crowd of movie-loving Christians flocked to streaming services and Walmart to buy my film that celebrated and validated their way of life. They did well. All of them got picked up and distributed by a major distributor and were loved by many. They starred old TV actors and movie stars, were seen by hundreds of thousands, and even trended on Netflix. I was finally not only paying my bills making and acting in films I created, I was getting accolades and praise from a crowd who showed me both their adoration and wallets.

I had slowly found myself a part of a community of filmmakers who proudly called themselves, "Christian filmmakers," who made what had now become a cultural genre called faith-based films. After the success of my first film, I remember waking up one morning to a message from one of the big-time Christian movie producers that said, "welcome to the club."

But something wasn't quite right. I had spent years writing and producing these "faith-based movies." I had received my pats on the back for making films that celebrated my beliefs while being "family-friendly." But somewhere, brewing deep in my heart, was a cloud of dissatisfaction threatening to break into a disruptive storm, lest I not heed its growing roar.

One night exactly a year before my first movie came out, I found myself in Universal Studios CityWalk, walking into a theater with some church friends to watch the newly-released Christian film. Over the next hour and a half, I took in the best art my faith currently had to offer. As the credits rolled, my heart sank, and for the first time, I felt that unsettling feeling. The movie was an embarrassing display of badly-crafted, poorly-acted, and shameless pandering propaganda. It failed to, in any meaningful way, capture the beauty of my faith, nor was it well-made by any filmmaking metric. It was touted as a "Christian movie," but in my estimation, it was hardly Christian and barely a movie. But whatever negative feelings I had got pushed down under a blanket of possibility when the news broke that it had made over 50 million dollars. The people had spoken, regardless of my and many other faithful art lovers' reservations. The movie was a hit. Perhaps I should've paid more heed to the depressing reality of what my faith had been reduced to, especially in the public square and cultural zeitgeist. But in seeing the booming box office, my youthful innocence found hope that there was an underserved market that wanted movies about faith — one that I could be a part of, and maybe they'd get better in the coming years.

So I made my own Christian movies and found success. I was right in believing there was a market, but as I continued to watch the landscape of faith-based films, I saw the money growing while the quality, depth, and beauty did not. There was a market, but it was one that would accept anything, no matter how badly made or poorly written, as long as it touted the audience's beliefs. But that was a hard truth for me to swallow when, after years of chasing my dreams, I was finally a working artist.

I once read an article about how the genre of films that have the largest return on investment are horror films and faith films, as neither have to be good to be consumed by their audiences. And somewhere in the middle of my journey as a faith-based filmmaker and actor, I found myself having an artistic and theological crisis of conscience. I grew up being exposed to both a beautiful view of faith and a high view of art. I was also shown how the two can and should intertwine to make even more meaningful and beautiful creations. I was taken to museums and concert halls around the world where I encountered the most renowned works of art, very often with subject matter from sacred scripture, where the artist's faith and love of God caused them to make more beautiful art instead of excusing subpar creations. Whether it was the Sistine Chapel painted with intricate detail and care across the walls of a church, or the Hallelujah Chorus sung in moving notes, rising to praise God, I was given a vision for just how beautiful faith could make our own creation. But finding myself in a club of "Christian artists" making bad art, I questioned if I should stay.

I had always loved movies and the power they had to inspire thought, evoke emotion, and probe the human condition. The medium had been so powerful in my own life that I believed, when infused with faith, it could actually bring us closer to God. But what I watched was a non-believing world laugh as we made shallow, low-quality movies, preaching to nobody but the choir, while Christians claimed persecution instead of making truly compelling art that might have the ability to reach a lost world in need. The mainstream Christian audience was more interested in "clean," "family friendly" escapism that reaffirmed their beliefs than they were in quality, deep, true, beautiful, human stories, like the ones we have seen throughout history. There were lines drawn around what the audience (and their dollar) would accept; the boundaries weren't based on quality, beauty, or even good theology – just puritanical moral rules and an unquestioned celebration of their beliefs, biases, and sometimes, even politics. They wanted propaganda that made them feel safe, not art that could change the world.

Early on, a secular distributor told me I needed to remove the word, "damn," from my movie, as Christians would get mad at foul language. Later, in audience reviews, there were multiple comments about my film (about a prodigal son) portraying alcohol. Then, I was surprised to find that a very popular watchdog Christian film reviewer on a large site had dinged my film for nudity because it contained a "girl in shorts." I was frustrated, but I was also learning what I could and could not do, portray, and say if I wanted to stay in "the club." I wanted to make movies like the ones that had touched me growing up, films that explored the human condition and illuminated even the darkest parts of life. But I also wanted to pay rent and continue living the dream of a successful artist I had fought so hard to realize. So every time I sat down to write a new film, I now sat with a whole audience looking over my shoulder, ready to turn their back on me with (literally) one wrong word. I tried my best at writing the stories I could love and believe in while staying inside the accepted lines, but I was writing with one hand tied behind my back.

It didn't happen all at once. It happened over multiple years of trial and failure, hope and reality, wisdom and experience, prayer and reflection. It took me orienting and ordering my priorities into what I believed God had called, not what the world (even the Christian one) wanted me to do. And it took me remembering the original, "why" I had begun – the "why" that had made me want to be in and make movies to begin with. It started with me trying to implement more human honesty into my stories, even if that meant selling less DVDs or receiving a few angry letters. It continued with me not resting on the crutch of sellable mediocrity, but putting time and effort into making my films more aesthetically beautiful, even when I had less money, resources, and support to do so. And it was completed when I released the article, "Why I Won't Make Another Christian Film," to the world and began production on the first movie I was artistically, and even theologically, proud of.

The movie was called *Don't Know Jack*. It was dark and brooding, it asked questions that didn't have easy answers, and it even had swear words. It was my film of freedom and the first one I actually felt reflected the kind of story I've always wanted to tell: a deep and meaningful one, told in a beautiful way, outside the stringent bounds of a tribalistic and fickle audience. Unsurprisingly, of all my films, it was made on the lowest budget, with the fewest resources, as it wasn't the kind of movie my previous audience could support. It made it into very few festivals and got no distribution offers. And when it was released, hardly anyone saw it. There were no applauding audiences, raving reviews, or church showings. But suddenly, all of that didn't matter. I had made something beautiful and true, and for the first time since I began my journey, I felt I had been a part of bringing something to life in a way that God had called me to.

I do sometimes miss the attention from an approving audience, the assurance of money, and the support from a "club." But now, I'd never trade the knowledge that I'm living out who I'm supposed to be with the hollow feeling of being praised for something I never was. It's a sacrifice, taking the road less traveled. But I'd like to affect one person in a long-lasting and meaningful way over the eyes of a million who will forget it in a day.

Chapter 23

Jesus in LA

"I am with you always, even to the end of the age."
- Jesus

I remember sitting in a popular and rowdy Hollywood bar on Sunset Boulevard one September night, a month after moving to town. The air was thick with fog and the sounds of thumping music vibrated through the packed space. I sat with a small group of people around a table, trying to have conversation over the deafening music, putting our heads close and raising our voices to yelling just so we could hear each other. The space was filled with what looked to be well over a hundred young, pretty people looking for attention, each with a drink in their hand and a smile across their face. The girls adjusted their tight tops and looked to and fro for whose eye they could catch. The guys strutted around the with the confidence of peacocks during mating season, looking for vulnerable targets who would validate their manhood. I came because I wanted friends, I wanted to fit in, and I wanted to "have a good time," but after an hour in the nonstop noise, I needed a breath. I stepped out into the tepid Hollywood night air, and took a deep breath. I gazed down the boulevard at the flashing lights and the expensive cars full of laughing people, whizzing by. But as I turned my head back, I saw an unusual sight: down the sidewalk, walking towards me, was Jesus — no, really. He was garbed in a long white robe, had flowing brown hair and the beard to match. Seeing Superman, one of the Transformers, or a celebrity impersonator was a pretty common occurrence on Hollywood Boulevard, but seeing Jesus in the midst of all the madness was out of the ordinary. The Jesus figure walked, laughing at the comments and balking stares from strangers passing by in cars and on the sidewalk. As he walked by me, our eyes met. He smiled, then continued his way into the night.

It wasn't the real Jesus I saw that night. It was instead a man that TMZ named as Kevin Short, who became known as, "West Hollywood Jesus." Kevin spent years walking around Hollywood, taking pictures with tourists, and telling people they were loved and special. I don't know why Kevin did this. But his presence ultimately struck a deep chord with many people through his cosplaying years. A few years back, Kevin regrettably died. He left behind him many mourners who shared their meaningful interactions with him online. I knew when I saw Kevin that he wasn't actually Jesus, but still, the visual of my Savior appearing in such a dark and lonely place struck a chord with me and burned an image in my mind I'll not soon forget.

~

I often think about the real Jesus coming to Los Angeles. I picture him in a pair of old jeans, a white T-shirt, and flip flops, walking through flashing lights and crowds of Hollywood tourists hoping to catch a glimpse of someone famous. I see him wandering down Sunset Boulevard, past the strip clubs, with their neon lights reflecting off his tan skin, as he makes his way downtown, where the streets are lined with homeless people hoping to catch a dollar from the passersby. I see him leaning against the outside wall of Paramount Studios as the young, small actors with big egos walk to their sports cars. I see him wandering the Hollywood Hills, past the wild parties raging into the night as vulnerable young hopefuls make decisions they'll regret for the rest of their lives, drowned out by thumping music and promises of fame. I see Jesus standing in the corner, right outside of the bright lights of a movie set, watching a new blockbuster being made. I see Jesus in the studio apartments of those like me, feeling left out, forgotten, lost, and hopeless.

I wonder what Jesus thinks in each of these places about each of these people. I wonder what he thinks about me. But I don't have to wonder much. In reading the words of his autobiography, I find Jesus in almost the same situations – with people acting the same way over two thousand years ago as they do today. We haven't changed much, so I imagine Jesus hasn't either. Jesus was the God who saw the homeless and touched them. He was the God who humanized the "sinful woman." Jesus was the man who humbled the proud for touting their money and status, and was angry at the powerful for exploiting the weak. Jesus was the One who stood in front of the woman caught in adultery and said, "Let you who is without sin cast the first stone." He was the One who offered a young, egocentric man a new life if he could only untie himself from his material identity.

~

There's a song I recently came across called "Jesus in LA." It's about the devil inviting the young and naïve into darker and darker places. In the chorus, the devil states, "You won't find Jesus in LA." And perhaps we all think this to be true. If you listen to the old fire and brimstone preachers, there's too much sin, ugliness, and depravity going on here for Jesus to show up. While I like the catchy tune and the poetic lyrics, I disagree with the author's conclusion. I've lived in Hollywood off and on for over a decade. I've seen the good, the bad, and the ugly. I've seen the dark sides of the bright city, and have found myself at the bottom of multiple barrels, relationships, bad choices, and dark moments. And I can assure you, Jesus was in all of them. If you listen to Jesus himself, you'll find him.

~

I don't live in Hollywood anymore. I escaped LA with my life and a wife to the other side of the country. I traded coasts and apartments, and now call myself a New Yorker. I left because my soul could no longer bear the weight of shadow that hung over the sunny city, living in every inch of its streets and every corner of every apartment. The smog that covered the city was filled with more than just pollution in the sky – it was full of anxiety and sadness from the people who lived below. I left because there came a time when I would wake up every day in Los Angeles with a panic attack, and to survive what many haven't, I knew I had to leave.

But Jesus didn't leave. And he won't. He won't leave until every little lost sheep is accounted for. He will walk the streets of Hollywood until every woman who has been taken advantage of is restored and healed; he will wander the alleys until every drug addict finally finds the peace they've been chasing; he will enter every movie set until the sad stories we tell are changed to hopeful ones; he will sit on every highway until you notice him.

Jesus is a God who comes – he came out of heaven to be born into a body to save a world that ultimately killed him. And he's a God who will never stop coming until you, his kid, let him love you. So rest assured, Jesus is and will always be in LA. And if you keep your eyes and heart peeled, you just might find God in Hollywood.

The End

Books by Nathan Clarkson

Wisdom Chasers: Catching Glimpses of the Divine in the Pursuit of Truth

Wonder Catchers: Thoughts, Prayers, and Poems, on Love, Life, and God

Different: The Story of an Outside-the-Box Kid and the Mom Who Loved Him

Good Man: An Honest Journey Into Discovering Who Men Were Actually Created to Be

The Way of Kings: Ancient Wisdom for the Modern Man

Only You Can Be You: What Makes You Different Makes You Great

The Clubhouse: Open the Door to Limitless Adventure

Films by Nathan Clarkson

Confessions of a Prodigal Son

The Unlikely Good Samaritan

Miracle on Highway 34

Don't Know Jack

Bright Sky

Connect with Nathan Clarkson

Website: www.nathanclarkson.me

Podcast: The Overthinkers

Instagram: @nathanjclarkson

Facebook: www.facebook.com/nathanclarkson

IMDb: www.imdb.me/nathanclarkson

YouTube: www.youtube.com/nathanclarkson

Email: nathanjclarkson@gmail.com